# vegan

*...made simple*

This edition published by Parragon Books Ltd in 2013 and distributed by

Parragon Inc.
440 Park Avenue South, 13th Floor
New York, NY 10016
www.parragon.com/lovefood

LOVE FOOD is an imprint of Parragon Books Ltd

ISBN 978-1-4723-4240-9

Printed in China

New recipes by Jane Hughes
Cover and new internal photography by Noel Murphy
Home economy for new photography by Penny Stephens

### Notes for the Reader
This book uses standard kitchen measuring spoons and cups. All spoon and cup measurements are level unless otherwise indicated. Unless otherwise stated, individual vegetables are medium, and pepper is freshly ground black pepper. Unless otherwise stated, all root vegetables should be washed and peeled before using.

Garnishes and serving suggestions are all optional and not necessarily included in the recipe ingredients or method. The times given are only an approximate guide. Preparation times differ according to the techniques used by different people and the cooking times may also vary from those given.

Pregnant and breast-feeding women are advised to avoid eating peanuts and peanut products. People with nut allergies should be aware that some of the prepared ingredients used in the recipes in this book may contain nuts. Always check the packaging before use.

The publisher recommends consulting a physician or other health-care professional before embarking on major dietary changes or introducing supplements to your diet if you have a chronic health problem, such as heart disease or diabetes. The publisher disclaims any liability, loss, or risk that may be claimed or incurred as consequence—directly or indirectly—of the use and/or application of any of the contents of this publication.

The publisher has been careful to select recipes that do not contain animal products. Any prepared ingredients that could contain animal products have been listed as "vegan," so readers know to look for the vegan version. However, always read labels carefully and, if necessary, check with the manufacturer.

# vegan
## ...made simple

# introduction

Veganism is moving into the mainstream. As more and more people have chosen to be vegetarian over the past decades, interest in veganism is also growing. Unlike vegetarians, vegans prefer not to consume any food or drink that is derived from an animal. The vegan diet is free from eggs, dairy foods, and even honey. In days gone by, critics of vegetarianism argued that the diet was not a healthy one and that, for the sake of our health, a balanced diet must include meat. Yet, today millions of vegetarians are thriving and research tells us that, far from being essential for our health, meat (and especially red and processed meat) is something we should aim to eat less, not more, of. For those who decide to eat less meat for either health or animal welfare reasons, being vegan is a logical step. Dairy foods are often high in fat and cholesterol, and the large-scale production of milk and eggs inevitably raises concerns about how we treat animals. The old arguments against vegetarianism, that it is a restrictive and unhealthy diet, are now leveled against veganism—but once again, the proof is in the eating. People report that moving to a plant-base diet has improved their health, that they feel

invigorated and fit, and that they can no longer understand why they once relied on dairy foods and eggs for protein. As the world's population rockets, we must find a way to feed everybody. The answer is not to build intensive dairy farms or to genetically engineer animals to yield more milk, more eggs, or more meat. The fact is that we do not need to eat food that comes from animals. If we continue to eat food from animals, it means using water and grains that could sustain many people to produce unhealthy animal-base foods that feed far fewer people. It's time to rethink our diets. A plant-base diet is sensible, healthy, and better for the planet. But we're only human and we eat for enjoyment as well as fuel. Divided into sections on breakfasts, snacks, lunches, dinners, and desserts, this book offers recipes for a variety of tasty dishes that everybody will enjoy. Yes, vegans can eat cake and ice cream at long last! Whether you're experimenting with vegan cuisine for the first time or looking for some fresh inspiration for an established vegan diet, these straightforward recipes are sure to become favorites.

# breakfast

# green apple & kiwi juice

## ingredients

*serves 2*

2 green apples, such as
  Granny Smith
½ cucumber
2 kiwis
½ lemon
¾-inch piece fresh ginger, peeled

## method

**1** Core the apples and then chop the unpeeled flesh into small pieces. Dice the cucumber. Peel the kiwis, using a standard vegetable peeler, then chop into small pieces. Cut the lemon into thin slices and set two slices to one side. Finely chop the ginger using a sharp knife.

**2** Place all of the ingredients into a juicer and juice all the ingredients together until all the liquid is extracted.

**3** Transfer the juice to tall glasses and decorate the glasses with the remaining lemon slices. Serve immediately.

# berry sunrise smoothie

## ingredients

*serves 1*

1 banana
2 ounces silken tofu, drained
¾ cup orange juice
2 cups frozen mixed berries

## method

1 Coarsely chop the banana and the tofu into smaller pieces.

2 Place all of the ingredients into a food processor or blender, or place into a large, deep bowl and use a handheld blender. Blend gently until thoroughly combined.

3 Serve immediately in a tall drinking glass.

# strawberry & vanilla soy shake

## ingredients

### serves 2

1½ cups strawberries
1 cup plain soy yogurt
½ cup chilled soy milk
2 teaspoons vanilla extract
agave nectar, to taste

## method

**1** Pick over the strawberries, then hull and halve them and place into a small bowl.

**2** Place the strawberry halves, yogurt, milk, and vanilla extract into a food processor or blender, or place these ingredients into a large, deep bowl and use a handheld blender. Blend gently until thoroughly combined. Sweeten with agave nectar to taste.

**3** Serve immediately in tall drinking glasses.

# apricot & ginger juice

## ingredients

*serves 2*

6 apricots
1 orange
1 fresh lemongrass stalk
¾-inch piece fresh ginger, peeled
ice cubes, to serve

## method

1 Halve and pit the apricots. Peel the orange, leaving some of the white pith. Cut the lemongrass into chunks.

2 Place the apricots, orange, lemongrass, and ginger in a juicer and juice all the ingredients together until all the liquid is extracted. Pour the mixture into glasses, add ice, and serve immediately.

# red pepper booster

## ingredients

*serves 2*

1 cup carrot juice
1 cup tomato juice
2 large red bell peppers, seeded
    and coarsely chopped
1 tablespoon lemon juice
pepper, to taste
lemon slices, to garnish

## method

1 Pour the carrot juice and tomato juice into a food processor or blender and process gently until combined.

2 Add the red bell peppers and lemon juice. Season with plenty of pepper and process until smooth. Pour the mixture into glasses, garnish with lemon slices, and serve immediately.

# maple & banana soy shake

## ingredients

*serves 2*

large banana
1½ cups soy or almond milk
2 tablespoons vegan
    omega 3-6-9 oil
1 teaspoon maple syrup

## method

**1** Chop the banana and place the pieces into a small bowl.

**2** Place the banana pieces, milk, and omega oil into a food processor or blender, or place these ingredients into a large, deep bowl and use a handheld blender. Blend gently until thoroughly combined. Sweeten with maple syrup to taste.

**3** Serve immediately in tall drinking glasses.

# peanut butter muesli

## ingredients

*serves 3–4*

1⅓ cups rolled oats
3 tablespoons flaxseed meal
    (ground flaxseeds)
2 tablespoons vegan margarine
3 tablespoons chunky
    peanut butter
2 tablespoons light agave nectar
½ teaspoon vanilla extract
soy milk or soy yogurt and
    blueberries, to serve

## method

1 Preheat the oven to 325°F. Line a baking sheet with parchment paper.

2 Mix together the oats and flaxseed meal in a large bowl.

3 Warm the margarine, peanut butter, and agave nectar together, either in a small saucepan over low heat or in a heatproof bowl in the microwave, until the margarine melts. Add the vanilla extract and mix together thoroughly.

4 Stir the liquid mixture into the oats and flaxseed meal in the bowl and stir well to combine.

5 Spread the oat mixture onto the prepared baking sheet and bake in the preheated oven for 20 minutes, or until dry and beginning to turn golden. Remove from the oven and let the mixture cool completely. Crumble up the muesli and store in an airtight container, or serve immediately in bowls with soy milk or soy yogurt and fresh blueberries.

# cherry almond granola

## ingredients

*serves 10*

1 spray of vegetable oil spray
2½ cups rolled oats
¾ cup dry unsweetened coconut
½ cup slivered almonds
½ cup flaxseed meal
   (ground flaxseeds)
¼ teaspoon salt
½ cup maple syrup
¼ cup water
1 tablespoon vegetable oil
1 teaspoon vanilla extract
⅔ cup chopped, pitted
   dried cherries
soy milk, to serve

## method

1 Preheat the oven to 275°F. Line a large baking sheet with parchment paper and spray it lightly with the vegetable oil spray.

2 In a large bowl, combine the oats, coconut, almonds, flaxseed meal, and salt and stir to mix well. In a small bowl, combine the maple syrup, water, vegetable oil, and vanilla extract. Pour the liquid mixture over the dry mixture and stir well. Pour the mixture onto the prepared baking sheet and spread out into an even layer.

3 Bake in the preheated oven for about 45 minutes, then stir well and spread out again into an even layer. Continue to bake for an additional 30–40 minutes, until crisp and beginning to brown. Stir in the cherries and let cool to room temperature.

4 Store in a tightly covered container for up to a week at room temperature or serve immediately with soy milk.

# coffee & walnut breakfast muffins

## ingredients

*makes 12*

vegan margarine, for greasing
2 cups all-purpose flour
1 tablespoon baking powder
2 tablespoons espresso powder
1 teaspoon cinnamon
¾ cup vegan granulated sugar
1 cup soy milk
⅓ cup canola oil
1 tablespoon vanilla extract
¾ cup chopped walnuts

### topping

¼ cup finely chopped walnuts
2 tablespoons packed vegan
  brown sugar

## method

1 Preheat the oven to 350°F. Lightly grease a muffin pan or place 12 muffin cups in a muffin pan.

2 Sift together the flour, baking powder, espresso powder, and cinnamon into a large bowl and stir in the granulated sugar.

3 Whisk together the soy milk, oil, and vanilla extract in a small bowl. Stir into the dry ingredients, adding the chopped walnuts at the same time. Mix until just combined—do not overmix.

4 Divide the batter among the cups of the prepared muffin pan and sprinkle the top of each muffin with the finely chopped walnuts and brown sugar. Bake in the preheated oven for 20–25 minutes, or until a toothpick inserted into a muffin comes out clean. Let cool slightly for 5 minutes before removing from the pan and serving.

# sunshine salad with muesli cookies

## ingredients

*makes 2 salads and*
  *30 cookies*

**fruit salad**
1 large orange
1 grapefruit
1 ruby grapefruit
maple syrup, to taste

**cookies**
¾ cup packed vegan margarine
1½ cups vegan granulated sugar
1⅓ cups all-purpose flour
½ teaspoon baking powder
⅓ cup flaxseed meal
    (ground flaxseeds)
1 teaspoon cinnamon
½ teaspoon salt
½ cup soy milk
1 teaspoon vanilla extract
⅓ cup raisins
⅓ cup finely chopped dates
½ cup finely chopped walnuts
2¾ cups rolled oats

## method

*1* Preheat the oven to 350°F. Line a large baking sheet with parchment paper.

*2* To make the cookies, cream together the margarine and sugar in a large mixing bowl until light and fluffy. Sift together the flour and baking powder and stir into the bowl with the flaxseed meal, cinnamon, and salt.

*3* Whisk together the soy milk and vanilla extract in a small bowl and stir into the mixture, adding the raisins, dates, walnuts, and oats at the same time. Mix until thoroughly combined.

*4* Roll a little of the cookie dough into a ball 1½ inches in diameter. Place on the prepared baking sheet and flatten slightly. Continue with the rest of the dough to make 30 small cookies. Bake in the preheated oven for 15 minutes, or until golden. Let cool on the sheet for 5 minutes, then transfer to a wire rack to cool completely.

*5* To make the salad, use a sharp knife to peel away all the skin and pith from the orange and grapefruits. Carefully cut V-shape wedges between each segment of the fruit to remove the flesh without the membranes. Divide the fruit between two small serving dishes and drizzle with maple syrup to taste. Serve each fruit salad with two or three cookies. (Store the remaining cookies in a container and consume within 5 days.)

# tropical oatmeal

## ingredients

*serves 2*

1 cup rolled oats
1¼ cups hot water
pinch of salt
⅓ cup tropical fruit and nut mix
1 large or 2 small bananas
coconut milk, to serve

## method

**1** Put the oats into a nonstick saucepan and add the hot water and salt. Stir well and bring to a boil, then reduce the heat and simmer, stirring often, for 5 minutes, until the oatmeal is thick and fairly smooth.

**2** When the oatmeal is nearly ready, stir in the tropical fruit and nut mix and cook for an additional minute.

**3** Spoon the oatmeal into two serving bowls. Peel the banana and slice it over the top. Serve immediately with coconut milk.

# herbed tofu scramble

## ingredients

*serves 2*

14 ounces firm tofu
12 cherry tomatoes
olive oil, for roasting
1 small vegan ciabatta loaf
2 tablespoons vegan margarine
2 garlic cloves, halved and bruised
⅓ cup chopped fresh mixed herbs
   (tarragon, chives, parsley)
salt and pepper, to taste
smoked paprika, to taste

## method

*1* Preheat the oven to 400°F. If the tofu is packed in water, drain it and press the tofu block between sheets of paper towels to remove as much water as possible. Gently crumble the tofu into a large bowl.

*2* Place the cherry tomatoes in a medium roasting pan and drizzle lightly with olive oil. Roast in the preheated oven for 5 minutes, or until warm and beginning to split.

*3* Cut the ciabatta loaf in half and slice each half lengthwise. Toast the bread slices lightly on both sides.

*4* Melt the margarine in a large skillet over medium heat. Sauté the garlic in the margarine for 1 minute, then remove the garlic from the skillet and discard.

*5* Put the tofu into the skillet over medium heat and sauté it in the garlic-infused oil, turning occasionally, for 3–4 minutes, or until just browning. Remove from the heat, stir in the fresh chopped herbs, and season with salt and pepper.

*6* Sprinkle the tofu scramble with smoked paprika. Serve the scramble immediately on the toasted ciabatta, with the roasted tomatoes on the side.

# mushrooms on bruschetta

## ingredients

*serves 4*

12 slices vegan baguette,
   each ½ inch thick, or
   2 individual vegan baguettes,
   cut lengthwise
3 tablespoons olive oil
2 garlic cloves, crushed
3½ cups sliced cremini mushrooms
8 ounces mixed wild mushrooms
2 teaspoons lemon juice
2 tablespoons chopped fresh
   flat-leaf parsley
salt and pepper, to taste

## method

1 Place the slices of baguette on a ridged grill pan and toast on both sides until browned. Reserve and keep warm.

2 Meanwhile, heat the oil in a skillet. Add the garlic and cook gently for a few seconds, then add the cremini mushrooms. Cook, stirring continuously, over high heat for 3 minutes. Add the wild mushrooms and cook for an additional 2 minutes. Stir in the lemon juice.

3 Season with salt and pepper and stir in the chopped parsley.

4 Spoon the mushroom mixture onto the warm toast and serve immediately.

# bean breakfast burritos

## ingredients

*serves 2*

### spicy beans

1 tablespoon olive oil
1 onion, finely chopped
1 green bell pepper, seeded and
    finely chopped
1 (15-ounce) can adzuki beans,
    drained and rinsed, or 2 cups
    cooked adzuki beans
1 tablespoon molasses
1 tablespoon maple syrup
1 teaspoon English mustard
½ teaspoon cinnamon
1 teaspoon tomato paste
1¾ cups water
salt and pepper, to taste

2 tablespoons vegetable oil
2 vegan sausages, defrosted
    if frozen
½ cup pineapple chunks
2 soft vegan tortillas (square ones
    if available)
1 handful fresh baby spinach
    leaves, shredded

## method

1 To make the spicy beans, heat the olive oil in a large saucepan over medium heat and sauté the onion and green bell pepper for 3 minutes, or until softened. Add the remaining ingredients for the spicy beans, bring to a boil, then reduce the heat and simmer for 30 minutes. Season with salt and pepper.

2 Heat the vegetable oil in a skillet over medium heat. Cook the sausages together with the pineapple chunks for 10 minutes, or until browned. Let cool a little and slice the sausages into bite-size pieces.

3 Divide the bean mixture between the two tortillas and spread to cover the whole surface. Cover the beans with a layer of shredded spinach.

4 Divide the pineapple and sausage pieces between the tortillas, arranging them in a line down the middle if your tortillas are circular, or along one edge if they are square. Roll the tortillas up as tightly as you can to create a spiral effect.

5 Using a serrated knife, slice the tortillas into two or three pieces. Serve immediately.

# spinach & sweet potato pancakes

## ingredients

*serves 4*

### pancakes
1 cup soy milk
⅓ cup all-purpose flour
½ cup chickpea (besan) flour
1 small sweet potato, grated
1 small red onion, finely chopped
vegetable oil, for frying

### filling
1 (5-6-ounce) package fresh baby
    spinach leaves, shredded
2 tablespoons dried currants
1 tablespoon olive oil
¼ cup pine nuts
salt and pepper, to taste

## method

1 To make the filling, place the spinach in a saucepan over medium heat. Add a splash of water and cook for about 2–3 minutes, or until wilted. Turn out onto a plate, then blot firmly with paper towels to squeeze out as much water as possible. Set aside.

2 To make the pancakes, whisk together the milk, all-purpose flour, and chickpea flour in a large bowl. Stir in the sweet potato and onion, and mix thoroughly.

3 Heat a small amount of vegetable oil in a large skillet over high heat and pour one-quarter of the pancake batter into the skillet, using the back of a spoon to spread the batter out to the edges of the skillet. Cook for 2–3 minutes on each side, turning carefully, until brown and crisp. Transfer to a plate lined with paper towels and make three more pancakes.

4 Return the spinach to the saucepan with the currants, olive oil, and pine nuts and place over medium heat. Season with salt and pepper and cook for a minute or until heated through. Take one-quarter of the spinach mixture and place on one-half of a pancake. Fold over the other half. Repeat with the remaining pancakes.

## variation
Use the pancake batter to make 8–10 mini pancakes and serve as stacks, alternating pancakes with the filling.

# raw buckwheat & almond oatmeal

## ingredients

*serves 6*

**almond milk**

½ cup whole raw almonds,
    soaked overnight in water
1¼ cups water

**oatmeal**

2 cups raw buckwheat groats,
    soaked in cold water for
    90 minutes
1 teaspoon cinnamon
2 tablespoons light agave nectar,
    plus extra to serve
sliced strawberries, to serve

## method

*1* To make the almond milk, drain the almonds and transfer to a blender or food processor. Blend the almonds with the water. Keep the blender running for a minute or two to break down the almonds as much as possible.

*2* Pour the mixture into a strainer lined with cheesecloth and squeeze through as much of the liquid as possible into a large bowl or liquid measuring cup. You should get approximately 1¼ cups of raw almond milk.

*3* Rinse the soaked buckwheat thoroughly in cold water. Transfer to the blender or food processor with the almond milk, cinnamon, and agave nectar. Blend to a slightly coarse texture.

*4* Chill the mixture for at least 30 minutes or overnight. It can be stored, covered, in the refrigerator for 3 days.

*5* Serve in small bowls, topped with strawberries and extra agave nectar.

# snacks

# nutty toffee popcorn

## ingredients

*serves 2*

3 tablespoons vegan margarine
3 tablespoons packed vegan
   brown sugar
1 tablespoon light corn syrup
½ cup cashew nuts
⅓ cup popping corn
1 tablespoon vegetable oil

## method

**1** Place the margarine, sugar, and corn syrup in a saucepan over medium heat. Bring the temperature up to high and stir continuously for 2 minutes, then remove from the heat and set aside.

**2** Toast the cashew nuts in a dry, heavy saucepan over medium heat for 3–4 minutes, stirring frequently, until they begin to turn golden brown. Remove from the heat and transfer to a plate.

**3** In a large, lidded saucepan, stir the popping corn together with the oil until it is well coated. Put the lid on the pan and place over medium heat. Listen for popping and turn the heat to low. Shake the pan occasionally, holding the lid down firmly. Do not lift the lid until the popping has finished. Remove from the heat when the kernels stop popping.

**4** While the popcorn is still warm, stir in the toasted cashew nuts. Pour the toffee sauce over the top and stir well to coat the popcorn. Transfer the popcorn to a baking sheet lined with parchment paper and let cool before serving.

# maple-nut granola bars

## ingredients

### makes 12

1 spray of vegetable oil spray
1¾ cups rolled oats
½ cup chopped pecans
½ cup slivered almonds
½ cup maple syrup
¼ cup firmly packed vegan light
    brown sugar
¼ cup creamy peanut butter
1 teaspoon vanilla extract
¼ teaspoon salt
2 cups puffed rice cereal
¼ cup flaxseed meal
    (ground flaxseeds)

## method

1 Preheat the oven to 350°F. Coat a 9 x 13-inch baking pan with vegetable oil spray.

2 On a large, rimmed baking sheet, combine the oats, pecans, and almonds and toast in the preheated oven for 5–7 minutes, or until lightly browned.

3 Meanwhile, combine the maple syrup, brown sugar, and peanut butter in a small saucepan and bring to a boil over medium heat. Cook, stirring, for about 4–5 minutes, or until the mixture thickens slightly. Stir in the vanilla extract and salt.

4 When the oats and nuts are toasted, place them in a mixing bowl and add the rice cereal and flaxseed meal. Add the syrup mixture to the oat mixture and stir to combine. Spread the syrup-oat mixture into the prepared baking pan and chill in the refrigerator for at least 1 hour before cutting into 12 bars. Store in a tightly covered container at room temperature. Serve at room temperature.

# mocha cookies

## ingredients

*makes 14*

1 cup all-purpose flour
¼ teaspoon baking powder
3 tablespoons unsweetened
    cocoa powder
½ cup firmly packed vegan
    brown sugar
1 tablespoon espresso powder
½ cup packed vegan margarine
½ cup rolled oats

## method

1 Preheat the oven to 350°F. Line a large baking sheet with parchment paper.

2 Sift together the flour, baking powder, and cocoa powder in a large mixing bowl. Add the sugar and combine thoroughly.

3 Dissolve the espresso powder in 1 tablespoon of boiling water and stir into the bowl. Add the margarine and oats and mix thoroughly to form a soft dough.

4 Form the dough into 14 small balls, place on the prepared baking sheet, and flatten slightly. Leave spaces between the cookies, because they will expand during cooking. Bake in the preheated oven for 15 minutes, or until crisp. Transfer to a wire rack to cool, using a spatula. Let cool completely before serving or storing in an airtight jar for up to 5 days.

# lunchbox brownies

## ingredients

### makes 9

2 tablespoons flaxseed meal
(ground flaxseeds)
2 cups all-purpose flour
¼ teaspoon baking soda
½ cup unsweetened cocoa powder
1¼ cups firmly packed
vegan brown sugar
1 ounce vegan semisweet
chocolate
2 teaspoons vanilla extract
⅓ cup packed vegan margarine,
melted, plus extra for greasing
⅓ cup coarsely chopped
macadamia nuts

## method

1 Preheat the oven to 350°F. Grease and line an 8-inch square baking pan with parchment paper.

2 Mix the flaxseed meal with 3 tablespoons of water and set aside for 10 minutes.

3 Sift together the flour, baking soda, and cocoa powder in a large bowl. Add the sugar and combine thoroughly.

4 Break the chocolate into small pieces, place in a small bowl, and pour over ¼ cup of boiling water. Stir thoroughly to melt the chocolate.

5 Stir the flaxseed paste, melted chocolate, vanilla extract, melted margarine, and chopped nuts into the dry ingredients. Use your hands to form the mixture into a soft dough. Press the dough into the prepared baking pan.

6 Bake in the preheated oven for 30 minutes, or until crisp around the edges but the center is still soft. Carefully lift the brownie out of the pan using the lining paper, leave the paper on, and place on a wire rack to cool for 10 minutes. Carefully peel away the paper and cut into nine squares. Let cool completely before serving or storing in an airtight container for up to 5 days.

# mango & coconut muffins

## ingredients

*makes 10*

vegan margarine, for greasing
2 cups all-purpose flour
1 tablespoon baking powder
1 tablespoon flaxseed meal
   (ground flaxseeds)
¾ cup dry unsweetened coconut,
   plus 2 tablespoons for topping
⅔ cup vegan granulated sugar
9 cardamom pods
¾ cup soy milk
⅓ cup canola oil
1 fresh ripe mango, chopped

## method

1 Preheat the oven to 375°F. Lightly grease a muffin pan or place 10 muffin cups in a muffin pan.

2 Sift together the flour and baking powder into a large bowl. Mix in the flaxseed meal, coconut, and sugar.

3 Crush the cardamom pods and remove the seeds. Discard the green pods. Crush the seeds finely in a mortar and pestle or with a rolling pin and stir into the mixture.

4 Whisk together the soy milk and oil in a small bowl and stir into the mixture, adding the mango at the same time. Mix until just combined; do not overmix.

5 Divide the batter among the 10 cups of the prepared muffin pan and sprinkle the top of each muffin with a little of the extra coconut. Bake in the preheated oven for 25–30 minutes, or until a toothpick inserted into the center of a muffin comes out clean. Let cool for 5 minutes before removing from the pan. Serve or store in a cool place or refrigerator for 2–3 days.

# almond cupcakes

## ingredients

### makes 10

vegan margarine, for greasing
⅓ cup canola oil
¼ cup plain soy yogurt
⅔ cup soy milk
¾ cup vegan granulated sugar
3 tablespoons almond extract
½ cup ground almonds
   (almond meal)
1¼ cups all-purpose flour
1½ teaspoons baking powder
½ teaspoon salt

### icing

2 ounces vegan white or
   milk chocolate
¾ cup vegan confectioners' sugar
1½ tablespoons soy milk
toasted slivered almonds,
   to decorate

## method

**1** Preheat the oven to 350°F. Lightly grease a cupcake pan or line with 10 paper liners.

**2** Place the oil, yogurt, milk, sugar, almond extract, and ground almonds in a large mixing bowl. Sift in the flour, baking powder, and salt, then beat with an electric handheld mixture until the batter is well combined.

**3** Divide the batter among the cups of the prepared cupcake pan and bake in the preheated oven for 20–25 minutes, or until well risen and golden. Transfer the cupcakes to a wire rack and let cool completely before icing.

**4** To make the icing, melt the chocolate in a double-boiler or a large heatproof bowl set over a saucepan of simmering water. Remove from the heat and let cool slightly. Beat in the confectioners' sugar and soy milk and spread the icing over the cupcakes with a teaspoon while the icing is still a little warm and easy to spread. Top each cupcake with a few toasted slivered almonds.

# guacamole dip

## ingredients

*serves 4*

2 large avocados
juice of 1–2 limes
2 large garlic cloves, crushed
1 teaspoon mild chili powder,
    or to taste, plus extra to garnish
salt and pepper, to taste

## method

**1** Cut the avocados in half. Remove the pits and skin and discard.

**2** Place the avocado flesh in a food processor with the juice of 1 or 2 limes, according to taste. Add the garlic and chili powder and process until smooth.

**3** Season with salt and pepper. Transfer to a serving bowl, garnish with chili powder, and serve.

# raw cashew hummus

## ingredients

*serves 4*

1¼ cups cashew nuts
2 tablespoons tahini
juice of 2 lemons
¼ cup olive oil
½ teaspoon onion powder
½ teaspoon garlic powder
sea salt and pepper, to taste
paprika and chili oil, to serve
toasted vegan pita breads, to serve

## method

1 Soak the cashew nuts in a bowl of water for 2 hours.

2 Drain the nuts and place them in a blender or food processor with the tahini, lemon juice, olive oil, onion powder, and garlic powder. Process to a smooth paste. Gradually add a little water to adjust the consistency to suit your preference. Taste and adjust the seasoning with salt and pepper.

3 Transfer to a small dish and serve with a dusting of paprika, a drizzle of chili oil, and the toasted pita breads.

# eggplant pâté

## ingredients

*serves 6*

2 large eggplants
¼ cup extra virgin olive oil
2 garlic cloves, very finely chopped
¼ cup lemon juice
salt and pepper, to taste
2 tablespoons coarsely chopped
   fresh flat-leaf parsley,
   · to garnish
6 vegan crisp breads, to serve

## method

**1** Preheat the oven to 350°F. Score the skins of the eggplants with the point of a sharp knife, without piercing the flesh, and place them on a baking sheet. Bake in the preheated oven for 1¼ hours, or until soft.

**2** Remove the eggplants from the oven and let stand until cool enough to handle. Cut them in half and, using a spoon, scoop out the flesh into a bowl. Mash the flesh thoroughly.

**3** Gradually beat in the olive oil, then stir in the garlic and lemon juice. Season with salt and pepper. Cover with plastic wrap and store in the refrigerator until required. Garnish with the parsley and serve with crisp breads.

# salsa bean dip

## ingredients

*serves 4*

12 cherry tomatoes, quartered
1 small red onion, minced
1 cup canned adzuki beans, drained and rinsed, or 1 cup cooked adzuki beans
½ red bell pepper, seeded and finely chopped
½ or 1 red chile (to taste), seeded and minced
2 teaspoons tomato paste
1 teaspoon agave nectar
large handful of chopped fresh cilantro
salt and pepper, to taste
chili oil, to serve
4 small soft vegan tortillas, to serve

## method

1 Place the tomatoes, onion, beans, red bell pepper, chile, tomato paste, agave nectar, and cilantro in a large bowl. Mix together well and season with salt and pepper.

2 Cover the bowl and let stand in the refrigerator for at least 15 minutes to let the flavors develop. Preheat the broiler to medium.

3 Place the tortillas under the preheated broiler and lightly toast. Let cool slightly, then cut into slices.

4 Transfer the bean dip to a small serving bowl. Serve with the sliced tortillas and chili oil to dip.

# crispy zucchini crostini

## ingredients

**serves 6**

1 zucchini
1 teaspoon salt
½ Pippin apple, peeled and grated
1 tablespoon chopped fresh
    mint leaves
2 scallions, finely chopped
6 slices of vegan French bread
1 garlic clove, halved lengthwise
olive oil, to serve
pepper, to serve

## method

1 Trim the zucchini, grate coarsely, and spread over a clean, dry dish towel. Sprinkle with the salt and set aside for 5 minutes. Wrap the dish towel around the zucchini and squeeze to remove as much moisture as possible.

2 Transfer the zucchini to a large mixing bowl and stir in the apple, mint, and scallions.

3 Toast the bread slices lightly on both sides. Rub one side of each slice with the garlic halves.

4 Divide the zucchini mixture among the bread slices. Drizzle with a little olive oil and grind a little pepper over them before serving.

# sweet potato fries

## ingredients

*serves 4*

2 sprays of vegetable oil spray
6 sweet potatoes (about 2 pounds)
½ teaspoon salt
½ teaspoon ground cumin
¼ teaspoon cayenne pepper

## method

1 Preheat the oven to 450°F. Spray a large baking sheet with vegetable oil spray.

2 Peel the sweet potatoes and slice into ¼-inch thick spears about 3 inches long. Spread the sweet potatoes on the prepared baking sheet and spray them with vegetable oil spray.

3 In a small bowl, combine the salt, cumin, and cayenne pepper. Sprinkle the spice mixture evenly over the sweet potatoes and then toss to coat.

4 Spread the sweet potatoes out into a single layer and bake in the preheated oven for about 15–20 minutes or until cooked through and lightly browned. Serve hot.

# nachos with salsa & raita

## ingredients

*serves 4*

1 (7-ounce) package vegan lightly salted tortilla chips

### salsa verde

2 garlic cloves
1 tablespoon whole-grain mustard
2 tablespoons capers
¼ cup chopped fresh flat-leaf parsley
2 tablespoons chopped fresh mint leaves
2 tablespoons chopped fresh basil leaves
⅔ cup olive oil
1 tablespoon fresh lemon juice
salt and pepper, to taste

### cucumber raita

1 teaspoon cumin seeds
⅔ cup plain soy yogurt
¼ cucumber, peeled and grated
⅓ cup finely chopped, unpeeled cucumber
¼ teaspoon cayenne pepper

## method

**1** To make the salsa verde, place the garlic, mustard, capers, chopped herbs, ¼ cup of the olive oil and the lemon juice into a food processor. Process until the mixture is finely chopped. While keeping the machine running, gradually drizzle in the remaining olive oil. Season with salt and pepper. Chill for at least 30 minutes in the refrigerator before serving.

**2** To make the raita, dry-fry the cumin seeds in a dry, heavy skillet over high heat. Shake continuously for a minute or two, or until lightly toasted. Remove the seeds from the pan and crush them with a mortar and pestle or rolling pin. Place the yogurt, grated cucumber, chopped cucumber, and cayenne pepper in a large bowl, then add the toasted crushed cumin seeds. Stir until thoroughly mixed. Chill for at least 30 minutes in the refrigerator before serving.

**3** Serve the dips in small bowls with the tortilla chips on a large serving plate.

# vegetable pakoras

## ingredients

*serves 4*

⅓ cup chickpea (besan) flour
½ teaspoon salt
1 teaspoon chili powder
1 teaspoon baking powder
1½ teaspoons white cumin seeds
1 teaspoon pomegranate seeds
1¼ cups water
¼ bunch of fresh cilantro,
    finely chopped, plus extra
    sprigs to garnish
vegetables of your choice, such as:
    cauliflower, cut into small
    florets; onions, cut into rings;
    potatoes, sliced; eggplants,
    sliced; or fresh spinach leaves
vegetable oil, for deep-frying

## method

*1* Sift the chickpea flour into a large bowl. Add the salt, chili powder, baking powder, cumin, and pomegranate seeds and blend together well. Pour in the water and beat well to form a smooth batter. Add the chopped cilantro and mix well, then set aside.

*2* Dip the prepared vegetables into the batter, carefully shaking off any excess.

*3* Heat enough oil for deep-frying in a wok, deep-fat fryer, or a large, heavy saucepan until it reaches 350°F, or until a cube of bread browns in 30 seconds. Using tongs, place the battered vegetables in the oil and deep-fry, in batches, turning once.

*4* Repeat this process until all of the batter has been used. Transfer the battered vegetables to crumpled paper towels and drain thoroughly. Garnish with cilantro sprigs and serve immediately.

# lunch

# gazpacho soup

## ingredients

*serves 6*

5 fresh ripe tomatoes
10 sun-dried tomatoes in oil
½ red onion, chopped
2 garlic cloves
1 large handful fresh basil leaves
2 tablespoons olive oil
1 teaspoon vegan stock powder
2 tablespoons red wine vinegar
1 red bell pepper, seeded and
   finely chopped
½ cucumber, peeled and finely
   chopped
⅔ cup ice cubes
salt and pepper, to taste

## method

1 Place the fresh tomatoes, sun-dried tomatoes, onion, garlic, basil, olive oil, stock powder, and vinegar into a food processor or blender and process until smooth. Season with salt and pepper.

2 Transfer to a large bowl and stir in the red bell pepper, cucumber, and ice cubes. Chill thoroughly in the refrigerator before stirring well, check the seasoning again, and serve in small bowls.

# spicy zucchini & rice soup

## ingredients

*serves 4*

2 tablespoons vegetable oil
4 garlic cloves, thinly sliced
1 tablespoon mild red chili powder,
    or to taste
¼–½ teaspoon ground cumin
6⅓ cups vegan stock
2 zucchini, cut into bite-size chunks
¼ cup long-grain rice
salt and pepper, to taste
fresh oregano sprigs, to garnish
lime wedges, to serve

## method

1 Heat the oil in a heavy saucepan over medium heat. Add the garlic and cook for 2 minutes, or until softened. Add the chili powder and cumin and cook over medium–low heat for 1 minute.

2 Stir in the stock, zucchini, and rice, then cook over medium–high heat for 10 minutes, or until the zucchini is just tender and the rice is cooked through. Season with salt and pepper.

3 Ladle into warm bowls, garnish with oregano sprigs, and serve immediately with lime wedges.

# corn chowder

## ingredients

*serves 6*

1 tablespoon olive oil
1 onion, finely chopped
1 carrot, finely chopped
1 leek, finely chopped
2 garlic cloves, finely chopped
1 teaspoon dried thyme
1 tablespoon all-purpose flour
6⅓ cups vegan stock
1 sweet potato, finely chopped
3½ cups frozen corn kernels
salt and pepper, to taste

## method

1 Heat the oil in a large saucepan over low heat. Gently sauté the onion, carrot, leek, garlic, and thyme for 5–8 minutes, or until the onion is softened and translucent.

2 Stir in the flour and cook for an additional minute, then pour in the stock and stir well.

3 Add the sweet potato to the pan, bring to a boil, and then reduce the heat. Simmer for 20 minutes, stirring frequently, until the sweet potato is soft.

4 Stir in the corn kernels and cook for an additional 5 minutes.

5 Transfer 2 cups of the chowder to a food processor or blender. Blend until smooth and then return to the pan. Mix thoroughly and season with salt and pepper. Reheat the soup, then serve immediately.

# sweet potato soup

## ingredients

### serves 6

2 teaspoons vegetable oil
1 onion, diced
1 tablespoon finely chopped
   fresh ginger
1 tablespoon vegan Thai red
   curry paste
1 teaspoon salt
4 sweet potatoes, diced
1¾ cups canned coconut milk
4 cups vegan stock
juice of 1 lime
¾ cup finely chopped fresh
   cilantro, to garnish

## method

1 In a large, heavy saucepan, heat the oil over medium–high heat. Add the onion and ginger and cook, stirring, for about 5 minutes, or until soft. Add the curry paste and salt and cook, stirring, for an additional minute or so. Add the sweet potatoes, coconut milk, and stock and bring to a boil. Reduce the heat to medium and simmer, uncovered, for about 20 minutes, or until the sweet potatoes are soft.

2 Puree the soup, either in batches in a blender or food processor or using a handheld blender. Return the soup to the heat and bring back up to a simmer. Just before serving, stir in the lime juice. Serve hot, garnished with cilantro.

# thai vermicelli soup

## ingredients

### serves 4

½ ounce dried shiitake mushrooms
5 cups vegan stock
1 tablespoon peanut oil
4 scallions, sliced
10 baby corn, sliced
2 garlic cloves, crushed
2 fresh kaffir lime leaves, chopped
2 tablespoons vegan Thai red
     curry paste
3 ounces rice vermicelli noodles
1 tablespoon light soy sauce
2 tablespoons chopped fresh
     cilantro, to garnish

## method

1 Place the mushrooms in a bowl, cover with the stock, and let soak for 20 minutes.

2 Heat the peanut oil in a saucepan over medium heat. Add the scallions, baby corn, garlic, and kaffir lime leaves. Sauté for 3 minutes to soften.

3 Add the red curry paste and the soaked mushrooms and their soaking liquid. Bring to a boil and simmer for 5 minutes, stirring occasionally.

4 Add the noodles and soy sauce to the red curry mixture in the pan. Return the pan to a boil and simmer for an additional 4 minutes, until the noodles are just cooked. Ladle into warm bowls, garnish with the chopped cilantro, and serve immediately.

# maple-glazed tofu salad

## ingredients

*serves 4*

14 ounces firm tofu
1 tablespoon olive oil
½ cup pineapple juice
½ cup maple syrup
1 tablespoon soy sauce
2 tablespoons whole-grain
    mustard
mixed salad greens, to serve

## method

*1* Drain the tofu and press with paper towels to remove excess water. Cut into eight slices about ½ inch thick.

*2* Heat the oil in a large, heavy skillet over medium heat. Cook the tofu on both sides for 5–8 minutes, turning gently, or until browned.

*3* Meanwhile, put the pineapple juice, maple syrup, soy sauce, and mustard in a bowl and stir thoroughly to combine. Pour the mixture over the tofu in the skillet and reduce the heat to a simmer. Cook for 20 minutes, turning the tofu once.

*4* Serve the tofu slices warm or cold, on a bed of mixed salad greens.

# avocado & grapefruit salad

## ingredients

*serves 2*

1 ruby grapefruit, broken into
   segments
2 avocados, sliced
½ red onion, finely sliced
2 cups mixed salad greens

### dressing

4 dried dates, finely chopped
1 tablespoon olive oil
1 tablespoon walnut oil
1 tablespoon white wine vinegar

## method

**1** To make the dressing, combine the finely chopped dates with the olive oil, walnut oil, and white wine vinegar in a small bowl, using a fork.

**2** Place the grapefruit segments, avocado slices, and onion slices on a bed of fresh salad greens in a large salad bowl. Pour the dressing over the salad and toss, using two forks, to mix thoroughly. Serve immediately.

# chickpea & quinoa salad

## ingredients

### serves 4

⅓ cup red quinoa
1 red chile, seeded and finely
    chopped
8 scallions, chopped
3 tablespoons finely chopped
    fresh mint
2 tablespoons olive oil
2 tablespoons fresh lemon juice
⅓ cup chickpea (besan) flour
1 teaspoon ground cumin
½ teaspoon paprika
1 tablespoon vegetable oil
1 cup drained and rinsed,
    canned chickpeas

## method

1 Place the quinoa in a medium saucepan and cover
   with boiling water. Place over low heat and simmer for
   10 minutes, or until just cooked. Drain and refresh with
   cold water, drain again. Transfer to a large bowl and
   toss together with the red chile, scallion, and mint to
   mix thoroughly.

2 Combine the olive oil and lemon juice in a small bowl,
   using a fork.

3 Sift together the chickpea flour, cumin, and paprika
   into a wide, deep bowl. Place the vegetable oil in a
   medium skillet over medium heat. Roll the chickpeas
   in the spiced flour, then cook gently in the skillet,
   stirring frequently, for 2–3 minutes, letting the
   chickpeas brown in patches.

4 Stir the warm chickpeas into the quinoa mixture
   and quickly stir in the lemon-oil dressing. Serve
   warm or chilled.

# crunchy thai-style salad

## ingredients

### serves 4

1 slightly under ripe mango
5 romaine lettuce leaves,
    torn into pieces
1 cup bean sprouts
handful of fresh cilantro leaves
3 tablespoons crushed roasted
    unsalted peanuts

### dressing

juice of 1 lime
2 tablespoons light soy sauce
1 teaspoon vegan light
    brown sugar
1 shallot, thinly sliced
1 garlic clove, finely chopped
1 red Thai chile, seeded and
    thinly sliced
1 tablespoon chopped fresh mint

## method

1 To make the dressing, mix together the lime juice, soy sauce, and sugar in a bowl, then stir in the shallot, garlic, chile, and mint.

2 Peel the mango using a sharp knife or potato peeler. Slice the flesh from each side and around the pit. Thinly slice or shred the flesh.

3 Place the torn lettuce, bean sprouts, cilantro leaves, and mango in a serving bowl. Gently toss together. Spoon the dressing over the top, sprinkle with the peanuts, and serve immediately.

# bean & wild rice salad

## ingredients

*serves 6*

1 cup wild rice
1 cup drained and rinsed, canned kidney beans
1 cup drained and rinsed, canned great Northern beans
1 cup drained and rinsed, canned navy beans
1 red onion, thinly sliced
4 scallions, finely chopped
1 garlic clove, crushed

## dressing

¼ cup olive oil
2 tablespoons balsamic vinegar
1 teaspoon dried oregano

## method

1 Place the rice in a large saucepan, cover with water, and bring to a boil. Reduce the heat, then simmer for 45 minutes, or according to the package directions, until the rice is just tender and beginning to "pop." If necessary, add more boiling water as the rice cooks. When the rice is cooked, drain, refresh with cold water, and drain again.

2 To make the dressing, combine all the ingredients in a small bowl with a fork or small whisk.

3 Place all the beans in a large salad bowl with the onion, scallions, and garlic. Add the cooled rice and pour in the dressing. Mix together thoroughly, using a wooden or metal spoon. Chill in the refrigerator before serving.

# couscous with roasted tomatoes

## ingredients

*serves 6*

2 cups cherry tomatoes
3 tablespoons olive oil
¾ cup couscous
1 cup boiling water
¼ cup pine nuts, toasted
⅓ cup coarsely chopped mint
finely grated zest of 1 lemon
1½ tablespoons lemon juice
salt and pepper, to taste

## method

1 Preheat the oven to 425°F. Place the tomatoes and 1 tablespoon of the oil in an ovenproof dish. Toss together, then roast in the preheated oven for 7–8 minutes, until the tomatoes are soft and the skins have burst. Let stand for 5 minutes.

2 Put the couscous in a heatproof bowl. Pour the boiling water over the grains, cover, and let stand for 8–10 minutes, until soft and the liquid is absorbed. Fluff up with a fork.

3 Add the tomatoes and their juices, the pine nuts, mint, lemon zest, lemon juice, and the remaining oil to the couscous. Season with salt and pepper, then gently toss together. Serve warm or cold.

# ginger vegetable tempura

## ingredients

### serves 6

6 cups vegetable oil, for deep-frying

1¼ pounds fresh seasonal vegetables, cut into large pieces (such as bell peppers, snow peas, asparagus, broccoli, eggplants, zucchini)

1 tablespoon light corn syrup or maple syrup, to serve

1 tablespoon paprika, to serve

### ginger batter

2 cups all-purpose flour

2 cups cornstarch

1¼ cups club soda

1¼ cups sparkling vegan ginger beer or ginger ale

## method

*1* Preheat the oven to 325°F.

*2* To make the ginger batter, place the flour and cornstarch in a large, wide bowl. Slowly pour in the club soda and ginger beer or ginger ale, stirring quickly to create a smooth batter. If there are any lumps, stir again to remove.

*3* Heat the oil in a large saucepan or wok over high heat, until a drop of batter floats quickly to the top and sizzles. Dip each piece of vegetable in the batter, shake off the excess, and deep-fry for about 5 minutes, or until crisp and beginning to brown. Fry the vegetables in small batches, drain on paper towels, and keep on an ovenproof plate in the preheated oven while you finish the frying. Scoop out any stray pieces of batter from the oil between batches so that they do not burn and taint the oil.

*4* Serve the vegetables piled on a large serving plate, drizzled with the syrup and lightly dusted with paprika.

# layered tomato, pepper & basil

## ingredients

*serves 4*

1 teaspoon olive oil
2 shallots, finely chopped
2 garlic cloves, crushed
2 red bell peppers, peeled, seeded,
    and sliced into strips
1 orange bell pepper, peeled,
    seeded, and sliced into strips
4 tomatoes, thinly sliced
2 tablespoons shredded fresh basil,
    plus extra leaves to garnish
pepper, to taste

## method

1 Lightly brush four ramekin dishes with the oil. Mix
  the shallots and garlic together in a bowl and season
  with pepper.

2 Layer the red and orange bell peppers with the
  tomatoes in the prepared ramekin dishes, sprinkling
  each layer with the shallot mixture and shredded basil.
  When all the ingredients have been added, cover
  lightly with plastic wrap or parchment paper. Weigh
  down and let stand in the refrigerator for at least
  6 hours, or preferably overnight.

3 When ready to serve, remove the weights and carefully
  run a knife around the edges. Turn out onto serving
  plates and serve garnished with basil leaves.

# walnut pâté on ciabatta

## ingredients

*serves 4*

### walnut pâté

1 cup coarsely chopped walnuts

3 cups fresh whole-wheat vegan bread crumbs

1 small red onion, chopped

1 tablespoon chopped fresh tarragon

1 tablespoon chopped fresh chives

1 teaspoon tomato paste

1 teaspoon soy sauce

1 tablespoon vegan red wine (optional)

2 teaspoons walnut oil, plus extra as needed

salt and pepper, to taste

vegan ciabatta loaf, sliced, or crackers

## method

1 Place all the pâté ingredients in a large bowl and mix together well with a wooden spoon. Season with salt and pepper. Transfer to a food processor and blend until it forms a smooth paste. If the bread crumbs are dry, you may need to add a little more oil or red wine, if using.

2 Transfer the mixture to four small ramekin or similar dishes and chill in the refrigerator before serving. Serve the pâté with the slices of ciabatta or crackers.

# smoked tofu & vegetable baguette

## ingredients

*serves 2–4*

1 small zucchini, sliced
1 red or yellow bell pepper,
    seeded and sliced
1 red onion, cut into 8 pieces
2 tablespoons olive oil
14-inch vegan baguette
1 handful of fresh basil, chopped
1 handful of fresh arugula,
    chopped
3 ounces smoked tofu, sliced
½ tomato, sliced
1 tablespoon balsamic vinegar

### tapenade

12 ripe black olives, pitted and
    coarsely chopped
1 garlic clove
1 tablespoon olive oil
salt and pepper, to taste

## method

1 Preheat the oven to 375°F. Place the zucchini, bell pepper, and red onion on a baking sheet, drizzle with the olive oil, and toss together so that the vegetables are coated with the oil. Roast in the preheated oven for 25 minutes, or until softened and beginning to brown.

2 To make the tapenade, place the olives, garlic, and oil in a food processor and process to a rough paste. Season with salt and pepper.

3 Cut the baguette in half lengthwise and spread the cut side of the top half with the tapenade.

4 On the cut side of the bottom half, layer the roasted vegetables, including their oil, the basil, and arugula, then the tofu and tomatoes, and finally drizzle with the balsamic vinegar—the fillings will be piled high. Place the tapenade half on top and press down firmly to compress the filling.

5 Wrap the baguette tightly in plastic wrap or aluminum foil and refrigerate for at least an hour before serving. Slice carefully with a serrated knife into portions.

# mediterranean wrap

## ingredients

*serves 4*

1 small zucchini, thickly sliced
1 red or yellow bell pepper, seeded
and coarsely chopped
1 tablespoon olive oil
4 soft vegan flatbreads
⅓ cup tomato paste
3 cups fresh baby spinach leaves
4 artichoke hearts in oil, quartered
8 sun-dried tomatoes in oil,
quartered
16 ripe black olives, pitted
and halved
1 handful of fresh basil leaves, torn

## method

**1** Preheat the oven to 375°F. Place the zucchini and bell
pepper on a baking sheet, pour over the oil them,
and toss together so that the vegetables are well
coated. Roast the vegetables in the preheated oven
for 20 minutes, or until softened and beginning to
brown. Remove from the oven.

**2** Spread each flatbread with a thin layer of tomato paste.
Shred the spinach and divide it among the flatbreads.

**3** Mix the roasted vegetables together with the artichoke
hearts, sun-dried tomatoes, olives, and basil in a large
bowl. Divide the mixture among the flatbreads,
spreading the filling evenly on top of the shredded
spinach. Roll the flatbreads up tightly, slice in half, and
serve immediately.

# mushroom & pesto panini

## ingredients

### serves 2

2 tablespoons vegan margarine
3 cups sliced button mushrooms
1 onion, sliced
large handful of fresh flat-leaf
    parsley, chopped
1 vegan ciabatta loaf
olive oil, for brushing
salt and pepper, to taste

### pesto

½ cup cashew nuts
1 cup fresh basil leaves
2 garlic cloves, crushed
¼ cup olive or hemp oil
salt and pepper, to taste

## method

1 To make the pesto, lightly toast the cashew nuts in a dry, heavy saucepan until they begin to brown.

2 Place the toasted cashew nuts, basil, garlic, and oil into a food processor, season with salt and pepper, and pulse to a coarse paste. Alternatively, chop the cashew nuts and basil finely, and use a mortar and pestle to grind all the pesto ingredients to a paste.

3 Melt the margarine in a skillet over low heat and gently sauté the mushrooms, onion, and chopped parsley for 5 minutes, or until the onion is soft. Season with salt and pepper.

4 Slice the ciabatta loaf lengthwise and then slice each piece in half widthwise. Lightly brush the outsides of the bread slices with olive oil.

5 Divide the pesto into four portions and spread onto the cut side of each bread slice. Divide the warm mushroom mixture between two bread slices, then sandwich with the other two slices.

6 Heat a dry, ridged grill pan and cook the sandwiches for 2–3 minutes on each side, pressing down firmly to flatten them and produce grilled stripes.

# lunchtime bean burgers

## ingredients

*serves 4*

1 tablespoon sunflower oil,
plus extra for brushing
1 onion, finely chopped
1 garlic clove, finely chopped
1 teaspoon ground coriander
1 teaspoon ground cumin
2 cups finely chopped white
button mushrooms
1 (15-ounce) can cranberry or
red kidney beans, drained
and rinsed
2 tablespoons chopped fresh
flat-leaf parsley
all-purpose flour, for dusting
salt and pepper, to taste
vegan hamburger buns and salad,
to serve

## method

1 Heat the oil in a heavy skillet over medium heat. Add the onion and sauté, stirring frequently, for 5 minutes, or until softened. Add the garlic, coriander, and cumin and cook, stirring, for an additional minute. Add the mushrooms and cook, stirring frequently, for 4–5 minutes, until all the liquid has evaporated. Transfer to a bowl.

2 Put the beans in a small bowl and mash with a fork. Stir into the mushroom mixture with the parsley and season with salt and pepper.

3 Preheat the broiler to medium–high. Divide the mixture equally into four portions, dust lightly with flour, and shape into flat, round patties. Brush with oil and cook under the broiler for 4–5 minutes on each side. Serve in hamburger buns with salad.

# easy vegetable sushi

## ingredients

*serves 4–6*

1 cup glutinous rice
2–3 tablespoons Japanese
    rice vinegar
pinch of salt
1 tablespoon Japanese sweet rice
    wine (mirin)
7 sheets Japanese sushi nori,
    pretoasted
½ cucumber, cut into matchsticks
1 red bell pepper, seeded and cut
    into matchsticks
1 avocado, cut into matchsticks
4 scallions, halved lengthwise
soy sauce, wasabi paste, and
    pickled ginger, to serve
    (optional)

## method

1 Place the rice in a medium saucepan and cover with 1½ cups of water. Bring to a boil, then reduce the heat to low, cover, and let cook for 20 minutes, or cook according to the package directions. When cooked, drain the rice and transfer to a large bowl. Gently fold in the rice vinegar, salt, and mirin and let cool.

2 When the rice is cold, place one sheet of pretoasted nori onto a sushi rolling mat, shiny side down, and spread a thin layer of rice all over, leaving a ½-inch border along the far edge. Add a selection of the vegetable pieces, arranged in lines running the same way as the bamboo of the mat.

3 Use the mat to carefully lift the edge of the nori closest to you, roll it away from you, and tuck it in as tightly as you can. Continue to roll the nori up tightly and, if necessary, moisten the far edge with a little water to seal the roll together. Repeat with the remaining nori sheets, rice, and vegetables. Chill in the refrigerator, wrapped tightly in plastic wrap, until required. (You can do this step without a sushi mat, if you don't have one.)

4 To serve, cut each roll into slices about 1 inch thick. Serve with soy sauce and wasabi paste for dipping and pickled ginger as an accompaniment, if desired.

# stuffed potato skins

## ingredients

*serves 2*

vegetable oil, for greasing
2 baking potatoes
olive oil, for roasting and frying
3 vegan bacon-style strips
1 tablespoon chopped fresh mixed
    herbs, such as sage, parsley,
    oregano
½ tablespoon vegan margarine
salt and pepper, to taste

## method

1 Preheat the oven to 375°F and lightly grease a baking sheet.

2 Score a circle around each potato, in the place where you will eventually cut them in half. Wrap them in paper towels and microwave for 6–10 minutes, or until cooked through. Unwrap and let stand until cool enough to handle. Cut the potatoes in half and carefully scoop out the flesh, leaving a skin around ½ inch thick. Set the flesh aside in a medium bowl.

3 Rub the outside of the potato skins with olive oil and place them, cut side down, on the prepared baking sheet. Bake in the preheated oven for 15 minutes, or until browned, then remove from the oven and transfer to a clean baking sheet, cut side up.

4 Heat some olive oil in a skillet over medium heat. Cook the bacon for 5 minutes, or until crisp, and then chop finely or crumble them. Mash the reserved potato flesh with a fork, and then mix in the bacon and chopped herbs. Season with salt and pepper.

5 Preheat the broiler to high. Pile the mashed potato back into the potato skins, make ridges on top with a fork, and dot with a little vegan margarine. Place under the hot broiler for 5 minutes, until the tops are golden and crisp. Serve immediately.

# thai tofu cakes with chili dip

## ingredients

*serves 4*

10 ounces firm tofu,
  coarsely grated
1 lemongrass stalk, finely chopped
2 garlic cloves, chopped
1-inch piece fresh ginger, peeled
  and grated
2 kaffir lime leaves, finely chopped
  (optional)
2 shallots, finely chopped
2 fresh red chiles, seeded
  and finely chopped
¼ cup chopped fresh cilantro
¾ cup all-purpose flour,
  plus extra for dusting
½ teaspoon salt
vegetable oil, for cooking

### chili dip

3 tablespoons white distilled
  vinegar
2 scallions, finely sliced
1 tablespoon vegan
  granulated sugar
2 fresh red chiles,
  seeded and chopped
2 tablespoons chopped
  fresh cilantro
pinch of salt

## method

**1** To make the chili dip, mix all the ingredients together in a small serving bowl and set aside.

**2** Mix the tofu with the lemongrass, garlic, ginger, lime leaves, if using, shallots, chiles, and cilantro in a mixing bowl. Stir in the flour and salt to make a coarse, sticky paste. Cover and chill in the refrigerator for 1 hour, until the mixture is slightly firm.

**3** Form the mixture into eight large walnut-size balls and, using floured hands, flatten into circles. Heat enough oil to cover the bottom of a large, heavy skillet over medium heat. Cook the cakes in two batches, turning halfway through, for 4–6 minutes, or until golden brown. Drain on paper towels and serve warm with the chili dip.

## variation

If you prefer a milder dip, omit the chiles and flavor with Chinese five spice instead.

# roasted vegetable pizza

## ingredients

### makes two pizzas

1 green bell pepper, sliced
1 red or yellow bell pepper, sliced
1 zucchini, sliced
½ small eggplant, sliced
1 red onion, sliced
2 tablespoons olive oil,
    plus extra for the sauce,
    crust, and greasing
1 handful of fresh basil leaves, torn
1 handful of ripe black olives,
    halved
1 tablespoon pine nuts

### tomato sauce

1 onion, finely chopped
2 garlic cloves, crushed
2 cups chopped tomatoes
1 teaspoon vegan brown sugar
1 teaspoon tomato paste
1 teaspoon dried oregano
salt and pepper, to taste

### pizza crust

2¾ cups white bread flour, plus
    extra for dusting
1 tablespoon vegan
    granulated sugar
2¼ teaspoons active dry yeast

## method

1 Preheat the oven to 400°F. Lightly grease two baking sheets. Put the bell peppers, zucchini, eggplant, and red onion into a large bowl with the olive oil and mix well until coated with oil. Transfer to a roasting pan and roast for 30 minutes, or until just starting to brown. Remove from the oven and set aside.

2 To make the sauce, heat 1 tablespoon of oil in a large skillet. Sauté the onion for 4–5 minutes, then add the garlic and cook for an additional minute. Stir in the tomatoes, brown sugar, tomato paste, and oregano. Simmer gently for 6–8 minutes, until thick. Season with salt and pepper, then remove from the heat and let cool.

3 To make the pizza crust, sift together the flour, 1 teaspoon of salt, the sugar, and yeast in a large bowl. Stir in 2 tablespoons of oil and 1 cup of warm water. Turn the dough out onto a floured surface and knead for 8–10 minutes. Roll into two 10-inch circles and place on the two prepared sheets. Mix the basil into the sauce and spread evenly over the crusts. Top with the olives, vegetables, and pine nuts. Let rise in a warm place for 20 minutes. Increase the oven to 450°F. Bake for 10–12 minutes, or until golden brown. Let cool for 5 minutes, then serve.

# spicy black bean tacos

## ingredients

### serves 4

2 tablespoons olive oil
1 onion, thinly sliced
2 garlic cloves, finely chopped
1 green bell pepper,
   seeded and sliced
2 tablespoons tomato paste
2 tablespoons chipotle chili paste
   (or other chili paste)
1 (28-ounce) can black beans,
   drained and rinsed
1 tomato, coarsely chopped
8 vegan taco shells
3 cups shredded iceberg lettuce
1 avocado, sliced

## method

1 Preheat the oven to 350°F.

2 Heat the oil in a large skillet over medium heat. Sauté the onion, garlic, and green bell pepper for 5 minutes, or until the onion is softened and translucent. Stir in the tomato paste, chili paste, and black beans and cook for an additional 5 minutes. Stir in the chopped tomatoes and immediately remove from the heat.

3 Place the taco shells upside down on a baking sheet and warm in the preheated oven for 3 minutes.

4 Mix the lettuce and avocado together in a small bowl. Divide the mixture among the taco shells. Reheat the bean mixture, if necessary, and divide the mixture among the warm tacos. Serve immediately.

# quick ginger & miso stir-fry

## ingredients

*serves 2*

**sauce**

1 teaspoon miso paste dissolved in
   2 tablespoons boiling water
1 tablespoon tomato paste
1-inch piece fresh ginger, peeled

2 tablespoons vegetable oil
1 tablespoon sesame oil
1 green bell pepper, seeded and
   cut into matchsticks
1 red bell bell pepper, seeded and
   cut into matchsticks
¼ green cabbage, cored
   and thinly sliced
1 carrot, cut into matchsticks
1 red chile, seeded and finely
   chopped
6 scallions, finely chopped
⅓ cup edamame
   (green soybeans)
⅓ cup coarsely chopped
   cashew nuts
cooked rice or vegan noodles,
   to serve

## method

1 To make the sauce, mix together the warm miso and the tomato paste in a small bowl. Grate the ginger coarsely, then gather up the grated ginger and squeeze the juice into the miso mixture.

2 Heat the vegetable oil and sesame oil together in a large wok over high heat. Stir-fry the bell peppers, cabbage, carrot, chile, onions, edamame, and nuts for 5 minutes.

3 Stir in the miso-ginger sauce and cook for an additional minute.

4 Serve immediately, with rice or noodles.

# cornbread with spicy potatoes

## ingredients

*serves 6*

**spicy potatoes**

4 red-skinned potatoes, chopped
   in small pieces
2 tablespoons olive oil, plus extra
   for greasing
1 large onion, sliced
1 teaspoon dried thyme
¼ teaspoon turmeric
¼ teaspoon smoked paprika
¼ teaspoon salt

**cornbread**

2 cups soy milk
2 teaspoons cider vinegar
3⅓ cups cornmeal
1¼ cups all-purpose flour
2 teaspoons baking powder
½ teaspoon salt
⅓ cup canola oil
2 tablespoons maple syrup

chili oil, to serve

## method

1 To make the spicy potatoes, place the chopped potato in a medium saucepan of water over high heat. Boil for 10–15 minutes, or until cooked through, and drain. Heat the oil in a large skillet and sauté the potatoes, onion, thyme, spices, and salt for 8–10 minutes, or until golden.

2 Preheat the oven to 350°F. Grease an 8-inch round springform cake pan.

3 To make the cornbread, whisk together the soy milk and the vinegar in a medium bowl, and let stand for 5 minutes. In a large bowl, sift together the cornmeal, flour, baking powder, and salt.

4 Whisk the oil and maple syrup into the milk mixture, then pour into the dry ingredients. Mix the batter together thoroughly and spoon into the prepared cake pan.

5 Bake in the preheated oven for 25–30 minutes, or until lightly browned, and let cool for 5 minutes. Turn out onto a serving dish and top with the spiced potatoes, reheating them, if necessary. Top with a drizzle of chili oil before serving.

# dinner

# mushroom & spinach calzones

## ingredients

*makes 2 large calzones*

### dough
3 cups all-purpose flour,
  plus extra for dusting
1 teaspoon salt
1 tablespoon vegan
  granulated sugar
2¼ cups active dry yeast
2 tablespoons olive oil
1 cup warm water

### filling
2 tablespoons olive oil
2 onions, sliced
3 garlic cloves, finely chopped
8 ounces mixed mushrooms,
  coarsely chopped
2 tablespoons pine nuts
2 tablespoons vegan dry white
  wine
1 tablespoon chopped fresh basil
  leaves
1 (6-ounce) package fresh baby
  spinach leaves, shredded
salt and pepper, to taste

salad greens and sliced tomatoes,
  to serve

## method

*1* Preheat the oven to 375°F. Flour a large baking sheet.

*2* To make the filling, heat the oil in a large saucepan over medium heat. Sauté the onions, garlic, and mushrooms until the onions are soft and translucent. Stir in the pine nuts and the wine and cook for 2 minutes. Stir in the basil and spinach and cook for an additional 2 minutes, until the spinach is just wilted. Season with salt and pepper.

*3* To make the dough, mix together the flour, salt, sugar, and yeast in a large bowl. Stir in the oil and water. Turn the mixture onto a floured board and knead for 10 minutes, until smooth. Roll the dough into two 10½-inch circles.

*4* Divide the filling between the dough circles, placing it on one half of the circle and leaving a margin of 1½ inches around the edge. Fold the uncovered side of the dough over the filling and flatten the edges together, then use your fingers or a fork to fold and crimp the edges together.

*5* Transfer the calzones to the prepared baking sheet and bake in the preheated oven for 15–20 minutes, or until beginning to brown. Serve with salad and tomatoes.

# eggplant & chickpea penne

## ingredients

### serves 4

large pinch of saffron threads
2 cups vegan stock
2 tablespoons olive oil
1 large onion, coarsely chopped
1 teaspoon cumin seeds, crushed
¾ eggplant, diced
1 large red bell pepper, seeded
  and chopped
1 (14½-ounce) can diced tomatoes
  with garlic
1 teaspoon ground cinnamon
¾ cup fresh cilantro, leaves and
  stems separated and coarsely
  chopped
1 (15-ounce) can chickpeas,
  drained and rinsed
10 ounces vegan dried penne
salt and pepper, to taste
harissa or chili sauce, to serve

## method

**1** Toast the saffron threads in a dry skillet set over medium heat for 20–30 seconds, just until they begin to give off their aroma. Place in a small bowl and crumble with your fingers. Add 2 tablespoons of the hot stock and set aside to steep.

**2** Heat the oil in a large saucepan. Add the onion and sauté for 5–6 minutes, until golden brown. Add the cumin and sauté for an additional 20–30 seconds, then stir in the eggplant, red bell pepper, tomatoes, cinnamon, cilantro stems, saffron liquid, and remaining stock. Cover and simmer for 20 minutes.

**3** Add the chickpeas to the saucepan and season with salt and pepper. Simmer for an additional 5 minutes, removing the lid to reduce and thicken the sauce, if necessary.

**4** Meanwhile, bring a large, heavy saucepan of lightly salted water to a boil. Add the pasta, return to a boil, and cook according to the package directions, until tender but still firm to the bite. Drain and transfer to a warm serving bowl. Add the sauce and half the cilantro leaves, then toss. Garnish with the remaining cilantro and serve immediately with the harissa or chili sauce.

# mushroom & ale pot pies

## ingredients

### serves 2

1 tablespoon olive oil
3 cups sliced button mushrooms
1 onion, coarsely chopped
1 leek, sliced
3 tablespoons all-purpose flour,
    plus extra for dusting
1 cup vegan stock
1 cup vegan ale (dark beer)
1 teaspoon chopped fresh
    flat-leaf parsley
1 teaspoon soy sauce
salt and pepper, to taste
1 sheet vegan ready-to-bake
    puff pastry

## method

1 Preheat the oven to 375°F.

2 Heat the oil in a large saucepan over low heat. Sauté the mushrooms, onion, and leek for 10 minutes, or until the mushrooms have softened. Stir in the flour and cook for an additional minute, then gradually whisk in the stock and ale. Stir in the parsley and soy sauce and cook for an additional 10 minutes. Remove from the heat, check, and adjust the seasoning with salt and pepper, then let cool.

3 Place the puff pastry sheet on a floured surface and cut two oval or circular pie tops to fit two 1½-cup ramekins. Divide the cooled mushroom mixture between the ramekins, place the pastry lids on top, and transfer to the preheated oven. Bake for 15–20 minutes, or until the pastry is puffy and browned. Let cool for 5 minutes, then serve immediately.

# smoky bean chimichangas

## ingredients

### serves 4

2 tablespoons olive oil

2 onions, sliced

1 green bell pepper, seeded and sliced

1 red bell pepper, seeded and sliced

1 (15-ounce) can black beans, drained and rinsed

2 teaspoons chipotle chili paste

2 tablespoons vegetable oil, plus extra for frying

2 cups shredded kale

juice of 1 orange

4 large soft vegan tortillas

salt and pepper, to taste

cooked rice, to serve

carrot salad or salsa, to serve

## method

1 Heat the olive oil in a large skillet over medium–low heat. Sauté the onions and bell peppers for 10–12 minutes, or until the onions are translucent but the bell peppers are still firm. Stir in the drained beans and chipotle paste, cook for an additional minute, and then remove from the heat.

2 Heat the vegetable oil in a small wok over high heat. Stir-fry the shredded kale with the orange juice for 4 minutes, or until wilted. Season with salt and pepper.

3 Divide the cooked kale among the tortillas, making a neat pile in the middle of each flatbread. Top the greens with a layer of the bean mixture. Then carefully fold up the sides of the tortillas to make bundles.

4 Heat a small amount of vegetable oil in a large skillet over medium heat. Cook the chimichanga bundles briefly on both sides (starting with the side where the folds are visible) until crisp and golden. Serve immediately, with rice and salad or salsa on the side.

# spicy stuffed bell peppers

## ingredients

*serves 4*

4 bell peppers in assorted colors
3 sprays of olive oil spray
1 onion, finely chopped
2 garlic cloves, chopped
1-inch piece fresh ginger,
　　peeled and grated
1–2 fresh serrano chiles,
　　seeded and chopped
1 teaspoon ground cumin
1 teaspoon ground coriander
½ cup cooked brown
　　long-grain rice
1 cup shredded carrot
¾ cup shredded zucchini
3 tablespoons finely chopped
　　dried apricots
1 tablespoon chopped
　　fresh cilantro
⅔ cup water
pepper, to taste
fresh herbs, to garnish

## method

1 Preheat the oven to 375°F. Cut the tops off the bell peppers and reserve. Discard the seeds from each pepper. Place the bell peppers in a large bowl and cover with boiling water. Let soak for 10 minutes, then drain and reserve.

2 Place a large skillet over medium heat and spray with the oil. Add the onion, garlic, ginger, and chiles and sauté for 3 minutes, stirring frequently. Sprinkle in the ground spices and continue to cook for an additional 2 minutes.

3 Remove the skillet from the heat, stir in the rice, carrot, zucchini, apricots, and chopped cilantro, and season with pepper. Stir well, then use to stuff the bell peppers.

4 Place the stuffed peppers in an ovenproof dish large enough for the bell peppers to stand upright. Put the reserved tops in position. Pour the water around their bottoms, cover loosely with the lid or aluminum foil, and bake in the preheated oven for 25–30 minutes, or until piping hot. Serve garnished with herbs.

# asparagus & walnut lasagna

## ingredients

*serves 4*

6 ounces asparagus, trimmed
3 tablespoons olive oil
½ cup chopped scallions
2 garlic cloves, chopped
¼ cup all-purpose flour
3½ cups unsweetened soy milk
1 teaspoon soy sauce
¾ cup coarsely chopped walnuts,
    plus 1 tablespoon finely
    chopped
6 vegan dried lasagna noodles
salt and pepper, to taste

## method

1 Preheat the oven to 350°F.

2 Bring a large saucepan of salted water to a boil. Add the asparagus and boil for 6–10 minutes, until tender; do not overcook. Drain and refresh with cold water.

3 Heat the oil in a large skillet over medium heat. Sauté the scallions and garlic for 3 minutes, then stir in the flour and cook for an additional minute. Gradually add the soy milk, whisking continuously and keeping the mixture just on a boil. When all the soy milk has been added, boil for an additional minute or two until the mixture has thickened. Remove from the heat, stir in the soy sauce, and season with salt and pepper.

4 Arrange half of the asparagus in the bottom of a 9½ x 7-inch baking dish. Sprinkle half of the chopped walnuts on top, then pour one-third of the milk sauce over them. Cover with three lasagna noodles, then repeat with the remaining asparagus, chopped walnuts, and another third of the remaining sauce. Cover with the three remaining lasagna noodles. Finally, pour over the remaining sauce and sprinkle with the finely chopped walnuts. Season with pepper.

5 Bake in the preheated oven for 25 minutes, or until the lasagna noodles are cooked and the top of the dish begins to brown. Let cool for 5 minutes, then serve.

# sweet potato & lentil stew

## ingredients

### serves 4

2 tablespoons olive oil
2 sweet potatoes, cut into
   ½-inch cubes
1 onion, chopped
1 carrot, chopped
1 leek, sliced
1 bay leaf
½ cup green lentils
3 cups vegan stock
1 tablespoon chopped fresh sage
salt and pepper, to taste

## method

*1* Heat the oil in a large saucepan or stockpot over low heat. Gently sauté the sweet potatoes, onion, carrot, leek, and bay leaf for 5 minutes.

*2* Stir in the lentils, stock, and sage and bring to a boil. Reduce the heat and simmer for 20 minutes, or until the lentils are tender but not disintegrating.

*3* Season with salt and pepper, then remove and discard the bay leaf. Serve immediately.

# teriyaki tofu noodles

## ingredients

### serves 2

5 ounces vegan dried noodles
7 ounces firm tofu, drained
2 tablespoons sunflower oil or
   vegetable oil
1 red bell pepper, seeded and
   thinly sliced
12 baby corn, cut in half
   lengthwise
3 cups broccoli raab or
   Chinese-style cabbage
   (1½-inch pieces)
salt, to taste

### sauce

3 tablespoons tamari or
   dark soy sauce
3 tablespoons rice wine
2 tablespoons light agave nectar
1 tablespoon cornstarch
1 tablespoon finely grated
   fresh ginger
1–2 garlic cloves, crushed
1 cup water

## method

**1** Bring a large saucepan of lightly salted water to a boil. Add the noodles, bring back to a boil, and cook according to the package directions, until tender but still firm to the bite. Drain.

**2** Meanwhile, cut the tofu into ½-inch slices and then into bite-size pieces. Pat dry on plenty of paper towels. Heat a nonstick or well-seasoned skillet over medium–low heat, then add the tofu and cook for 3 minutes, without moving the pieces around the skillet, until golden brown underneath. Turn and cook for an additional 2–3 minutes on the other side. Transfer to a plate.

**3** To make the sauce, mix together the tamari, rice wine, agave, cornstarch, ginger, and garlic in a small bowl until well blended, then stir in the water. Set aside.

**4** Heat the oil in a wok or a large, heavy skillet. Add the bell pepper and baby corn and stir-fry for 3 minutes. Add the broccoli raab and stir-fry for an additional 2 minutes. Pour in the sauce and heat, stirring continuously, until it boils and thickens. Add the noodles and tofu and toss together over the heat for an additional 1–2 minutes, until heated through. Serve immediately.

# butternut squash spaghetti

## ingredients

*serves 4*

1 butternut squash, peeled,
seeded, and cut into
bite-size pieces
2 red onions, cut into wedges
1 tablespoon olive oil
15 sun-dried tomatoes in oil
12 ounces vegan dried spaghetti
salt and pepper, to taste
fresh basil leaves, to garnish

## method

*1* Preheat the oven to 350°F.

*2* Toss the butternut squash and onion together with
the olive oil. Place in a roasting pan and roast in the
preheated oven for 25–30 minutes, or until tender.
Let cool for 5 minutes.

*3* Cut the sun-dried tomatoes into small pieces and
stir into the roasted vegetables. Season with salt
and pepper.

*4* Bring a large saucepan of salted water to a boil.
Add the spaghetti, return to a boil, and cook for
8–10 minutes, or until tender but still firm to the bite.

*5* Drain the spaghetti well and divide among four warm
serving plates. Top with the vegetables and garnish
with fresh basil leaves. Serve immediately.

# bean & vegetable chili

## ingredients

### serves 4

¼ cup vegan stock
1 onion, coarsely chopped
1 green bell pepper, seeded and
  finely chopped
1 red bell pepper, seeded and
  finely chopped
1 teaspoon finely chopped garlic
1 teaspoon finely chopped fresh
  ginger
2 teaspoons ground cumin
½ teaspoon chili powder
2 tablespoons tomato paste
1 (14½-ounce) can diced tomatoes
1 (15-ounce) can kidney beans,
  drained and rinsed
1 (15-ounce) can black-eyed peas,
  drained and rinsed
salt and pepper, to taste
vegan tortilla chips, to serve

## method

1  Heat the stock in a large saucepan, add the onion and bell peppers, and simmer for 5 minutes, or until softened.

2  Stir in the garlic, ginger, cumin, chili powder, tomato paste, and tomatoes. Season with salt and pepper and simmer for 10 minutes.

3  Stir in the beans and peas and simmer for an additional 5 minutes, or until heated through. Serve immediately with tortilla chips.

# chickpea & cashew nut curry

## ingredients

### serves 4

1 cup diced potatoes
3 tablespoons vegetable oil
1 onion, chopped
2 garlic cloves, chopped
1¼-inch piece fresh ginger,
    peeled and finely chopped
1 teaspoon cumin seeds
1 teaspoon chili powder
½ teaspoon turmeric
½ teaspoon cinnamon
1 (15-ounce) can chickpeas,
    drained and rinsed
1 cup cashew nut halves
½ cup vegan stock
1¾ cups coconut milk
chopped fresh cilantro, to garnish
cooked rice, to serve

## method

1 Place the potatoes in a large saucepan of boiling water and cook for 10–15 minutes, until tender but still firm.

2 Heat the oil in a large saucepan over medium heat. Sauté the onion, garlic, ginger, cumin seeds, chili powder, turmeric, and cinnamon for 5 minutes, or until the onion is soft and translucent.

3 Stir in a boiled potatoes, chickpeas, and cashew nuts and cook for an additional 3 minutes. Stir in the stock and the coconut milk and stir to combine. Reduce the heat to low and continue to cook for 15 minutes, or until thick and creamy.

4 Garnish with cilantro and serve immediately with cooked rice.

# beet & seed risotto

## ingredients

### serves 6

6 raw, whole, even beets, unpeeled
2 tablespoons olive oil
1 onion, finely chopped
1 garlic clove, finely chopped
1⅓ cups risotto rice
3⅓ cups vegan stock
1 cup vegan dry white wine
salt and pepper, to taste

### topping

1 tablespoon caraway seeds
1 cup fresh white vegan bread
    crumbs
½ teaspoon vegan
    granulated sugar
1 tablespoon vegetable oil

## method

1 Place the beets in a large saucepan, cover with water, and bring to a boil. Cook for 45 minutes, or until the beets are soft and can be pierced with a fork. Drain in a colander and peel the beets under cold running water—you should be able to slide the skin off. Trim away any stubborn skin with a knife and set aside.

2 Preheat the oven to 350°F. Heat the oil in a large ovenproof casserole dish over medium heat. Sauté the onion and garlic for 3–4 minutes, or until translucent. Stir in the rice, stock, and ⅔ cup of the wine, cover, and transfer to the preheated oven. Cook for 30 minutes, until the rice is tender.

3 To make the topping, crush the caraway seeds with a rolling pin and then mix all the topping ingredients together in a small bowl. Transfer to a small skillet and sauté, stirring continuously, over medium heat for 2–3 minutes. Transfer the topping to a plate to cool.

4 Process about one-quarter of the beets to a smooth puree in a food processor. Chop the remaining beets finely. Stir the chopped and pureed beets into the risotto along with the remaining wine, and season with salt and pepper. Divide the risotto among six warm serving plates, sprinkle some of the crumbs on top of each, and serve immediately.

# wild mushroom fusilli

## ingredients

*serves 4*

1 pound vegan dried fusilli
½ cup hazelnuts
¼ cup olive oil
1 onion, chopped
4 garlic cloves, chopped
10 ounces mixed wild mushrooms
    (such as oyster or cremini),
    coarsely chopped
¼ cup finely chopped fresh
    flat-leaf parsley
salt and pepper, to taste

## method

1 Bring a large saucepan of lightly salted water to a boil. Add the fusilli, bring back to a boil, and cook according to the package directions, until tender but still firm to the bite.

2 Dry roast the hazelnuts in a small, heavy skillet for 3–4 minutes, or until the skins begin to brown. Turn them out of the skillet onto a damp, clean dish towel, fold the dish towel over the nuts, and roll them on the work surface to remove most of the skins. Chop the nuts coarsely.

3 Heat the oil in a large saucepan over medium heat. Sauté the onion, garlic, and mushrooms for 5 minutes, or until beginning to brown. Stir in the chopped nuts and continue to cook for another minute. Season with salt and pepper.

4 Drain the pasta and toss together with the mushroom mixture and the fresh parsley to mix thoroughly. Serve immediately.

# carrot sausage & mashed potatoes

## ingredients

*serves 4*

### sausages

1 tablespoon olive oil

2 scallions, chopped

1 garlic clove, chopped

½ fresh red chile, seeded
    and finely chopped

1 teaspoon ground cumin

4 cups shredded carrots
    (about 1 pound)

½ teaspoon salt

3 tablespoons chunky
    peanut butter

½ cup finely chopped fresh
    cilantro, plus extra to garnish

2 cups fresh whole-wheat vegan
    bread crumbs

all-purpose flour, for dusting

vegetable oil, for frying

### mashed potatoes

8 russet or Yukon gold potatoes
    (about 2 pounds), chopped

3 tablespoons unsweetened
    soy milk

¼ cup packed vegan margarine

salt and pepper, to taste

## method

**1** To make the sausages, heat the olive oil in a large saucepan over medium heat. Sauté the scallions, garlic, chile, and cumin for 2 minutes. Stir in the carrots and salt and mix well. Cover the pan and cook on low heat for 6–8 minutes, or until the carrots are tender.

**2** Transfer the carrot mixture to a large mixing bowl and mix in the peanut butter and cilantro, making sure that the ingredients are thoroughly combined. Let the mixture cool, and then mix in the bread crumbs.

**3** On a floured surface, form the mixture into eight large link-style sausages. Let chill in the refrigerator for up to an hour. Heat the vegetable oil in a skillet over medium heat and cook the sausages gently for 10 minutes, turning occasionally, until browned.

**4** Meanwhile, bring a large saucepan of lightly salted water to a boil. Add the potatoes, bring back to a boil, and cook for 15–20 minutes, or until cooked through. Transfer to a mixing bowl, add the milk and vegan margarine, and mash the mixture thoroughly until all lumps are removed. Season with salt and pepper.

**5** Place the mashed potatoes on warm plates and top with the sausages. Garnish with cilantro and serve.

# thai red curry

## ingredients

*serves 4*

2 tablespoons peanut oil or
    vegetable oil
2 onions, thinly sliced
1 bunch of fine asparagus spears
1¾ cups coconut milk
2 tablespoons vegan Thai
    red curry paste
3 fresh kaffir lime leaves
1 (6-8 ounce) baby spinach leaves
2 heads bok choy, chopped
1 small head napa cabbage,
    shredded
handful of fresh cilantro, chopped
cooked rice, to serve

## method

**1** Heat a wok over medium–high heat and add the oil. Add the onions and asparagus and stir-fry for 1–2 minutes.

**2** Add the coconut milk, curry paste, and lime leaves and bring gently to a boil, stirring occasionally.

**3** Add the spinach, bok choy, and napa cabbage and cook, stirring, for 2–3 minutes, until wilted. Add the cilantro and stir well. Serve immediately with freshly cooked rice.

# potato, broccoli & peanut casserole

## ingredients

### serves 4

1 pound new potatoes, sliced
1 tablespoon olive oil
½ small onion, finely chopped
1¾ cups coconut milk
½ cup chunky peanut butter
1 tablespoon soy sauce
2 teaspoons vegan
    granulated sugar
½ teaspoon crushed
    red pepper flakes
3 cups broccoli florets
½ cup unsalted peanuts
2 teaspoons vegan margarine,
    melted
salt and pepper, to taste

## method

1 Preheat the oven to 375°F.

2 Bring a large saucepan of lightly salted water to a boil. Add the potatoes, bring back to a boil, and cook for 8–10 minutes, or until slightly softened. Drain and set aside.

3 Heat the oil in a saucepan over medium heat. Sauté the onion for 2 minutes, then stir in the coconut milk, peanut butter, soy sauce, sugar, and red pepper flakes. Bring to a boil and stir well to be sure the ingredients are well combined. Reduce the heat and simmer for 5 minutes.

4 Meanwhile, place the broccoli in a steamer and lightly steam for 4–5 minutes, or until just tender.

5 Stir the broccoli and peanuts into the sauce, season with salt and pepper, and transfer to a wide, square baking dish.

6 Cover the mixture with the cooked potato slices, dot with the melted margarine, and season with pepper. Bake in the preheated oven for 20–25 minutes, or until the potatoes are browned. Let cool for 5 minutes before serving.

# kale & artichoke gnocchi

## ingredients

### serves 4

3 cups shredded kale
2 tablespoons olive oil
1 onion, chopped
1 (14-ounce) can artichoke hearts,
    drained and quartered
2 garlic cloves, chopped
1 teaspoon crushed
    red pepper flakes
juice of ½ lemon
2 tablespoons pine nuts
salt, to taste

### gnocchi

6 even-size baking potatoes
    (about 1½ pounds)
2 cups all-purpose flour,
    plus extra for dusting
2 tablespoons olive oil

## method

1 To make the gnocchi, preheat the oven to 450°F. Place the potatoes on a baking sheet and bake until fluffy all the way through—45 minutes to an hour, depending on the size of the potatoes. Let cool, then peel and mash the flesh with a potato ricer or masher, until very smooth. There should be no lumps.

2 Turn out the mashed potatoes onto a floured board and knead, working in the flour and oil, for 5 minutes. Divide the mixture into four and roll each into a long snake. Use a knife to cut into pieces about ¾ inch long.

3 Bring a large saucepan of salted water to a boil. Add the kale, return to a boil, and cook for 6–8 minutes. Drain and firmly press out any excess water.

4 Heat the oil in a skillet over high heat. Add the onion and sauté for 3 minutes, then stir in the artichokes, garlic, and red pepper flakes. Cook for an additional minute, then stir in the kale, lemon juice, and pine nuts. Set aside.

5 Bring a large saucepan of salted water to a boil. Add a small batch of the gnocchi, return to a boil, and cook for 2–3 minutes, until they float on the surface of the water. Continue to cook batches of the remaining gnocchi in the same way. Mix the gnocchi thoroughly with the kale mixture and serve immediately.

# raw shoots & seeds super salad

## ingredients

*serves 6*

2–3 cups mixed seed and bean
   sprouts (such as alfalfa, mung
   beans, soybeans, adzuki beans,
   chickpeas, and radish seeds)
3 tablespoons pumpkin seeds
3 tablespoons sunflower seeds
3 tablespoons sesame seeds
1 small Pippin apple
½ cup dried apricots
grated rind and juice of 1 lemon
½ cup coarsely chopped walnuts
2 tablespoons vegan
   omega-rich oil

## method

1 In a large mixing bowl, combine the sprouts and seeds.
Core and chop the apple and chop the apricots into
small pieces. Stir the fruit into the bowl, then stir in the
lemon rind and walnuts.

2 Make a dressing by mixing the lemon juice with the oil
in a small bowl, using a fork to thoroughly combine.

3 Stir the dressing into the salad and serve immediately.

# sichuan mixed vegetables

## ingredients

*serves 4*

2 tablespoons chili oil
4 garlic cloves, crushed
2-inch piece fresh ginger,
    peeled and grated
4 carrots, cut into thin strips
1 red bell pepper, seeded and
    cut into thin strips
6 ounces shiitake mushrooms,
    sliced
2 cups snow peas
3 tablespoons soy sauce
3 tablespoons chunky
    peanut butter
3½ cups bean sprouts
cooked rice, to serve

## method

*1* Heat the chili oil in a preheated wok and sauté the garlic, ginger, and carrots for 3 minutes. Add the red bell pepper and stir-fry for another 2 minutes.

*2* Add the mushrooms and snow peas and stir-fry for 1 minute.

*3* In a small bowl, mix together the soy sauce and peanut butter until combined.

*4* Using a wooden spoon, make a space in the center of the stir-fried vegetables so that the bottom of the wok is visible. Pour in the sauce and bring to a boil, stirring all the time until it starts to thicken. Add the bean sprouts and toss the vegetables to coat thoroughly with the sauce.

*5* Transfer to a serving dish and serve immediately with freshly cooked rice.

# golden vegetable casserole

## ingredients

### serves 4

2 tablespoons olive oil
1½ cups chopped butternut squash
1 sweet potato, chopped
1 onion, chopped
2 carrots, sliced
1 teaspoon cinnamon
¼ teaspoon turmeric
2½ cups vegan stock
6 baby corn, halved lengthwise

## topping

⅓ cup packed vegan margarine
¾ cup all-purpose flour
½ cup coarsely chopped walnuts
¼ cup rolled oats
salt and pepper, to taste

## method

1 Preheat the oven to 400°F.

2 Heat the oil in a large saucepan over medium heat. Sauté the butternut squash, sweet potato, onion, and carrots for 5 minutes. Stir in the cinnamon and turmeric and cook for an additional 2 minutes. Pour in the stock, reduce the heat, and simmer, stirring frequently, for 10 minutes. Stir in the baby corn.

3 To make the crumb topping, rub the margarine into the flour in a mixing bowl, until it forms a bread crumb consistency. Stir in the walnuts and oats until mixed thoroughly then season with salt and pepper.

4 Transfer the vegetables into an 8-inch square baking dish. Top with the crumb mixture and bake in the preheated oven for 20 minutes, or until warmed through and golden. Let cool for 5 minutes, then serve immediately.

# barbecue tofu kebabs

## ingredients

### *makes 6*

14 ounces firm tofu
3 red onions, quartered
12 button mushrooms

### marinade

1 cup tomato puree or
    tomato sauce
3 tablespoons cider vinegar
2 tablespoons packed
    vegan dark brown sugar
2 garlic cloves, finely chopped
¼ teaspoon salt
¼ teaspoon chili powder
¼ teaspoon smoked paprika

## method

*1* To make the barbecue marinade, combine all of the ingredients in a saucepan, stir, and place over low heat. Simmer for 10 minutes.

*2* Drain the tofu and press it with paper towels to remove any excess water. Cut it into nine squares, then cut each square in half to make 18 pieces.

*3* Arrange the tofu pieces, onion pieces, and mushrooms in a large baking dish and pour the warm marinade over them. Stir the mixture carefully to be sure that everything is well coated, but be careful to avoid breaking the tofu. Cover and let cool. Refrigerate the mixture until needed, but let the tofu and vegetables marinate for at least 2 hours.

*4* Preheat the broiler to high. If you are using wooden skewers, presoak them in water for 10 minutes before making up the kebabs. Thread two mushrooms, two pieces of onion, and three pieces of tofu onto six presoaked wooden skewers. Baste with the remaining sauce and place under the preheated broiler or on a barbecue, turning occasionally, until well browned and sizzling. Serve immediately.

# chunky lentil & brazil nut roast

## ingredients

*serves 6*

vegan margarine, for greasing
1 cup red lentils (available in
    health food stores)
1 bay leaf
2 tablespoons olive oil
1 onion, finely chopped
2 garlic cloves, finely chopped
1 carrot, finely chopped
2 cups Brazil nuts
1 tablespoon tomato paste
1 tablespoon soy sauce
3 cups fresh white vegan
    bread crumbs
1 tablespoon dried oregano
steamed green vegetables, to serve

## method

*1* Preheat the oven to 375°F. Grease and line a 9-inch loaf pan.

*2* Place the lentils and bay leaf in a large saucepan with 1½ cups of water. Bring to a boil and then simmer for 25 minutes, or until the lentils are cooked to a mush. Remove and discard the bay leaf and set aside.

*3* Heat the oil in a large skillet over medium heat. Sauté the onion, garlic, and carrot for 3 minutes. Coarsely chop one-third of the Brazil nuts. Place the remaining nuts in a food processor and pulse until processed to a powder. Transfer the onion mixture into a large mixing bowl with the ground and chopped nuts, lentils, tomato paste, soy sauce, bread crumbs, and oregano. Mix thoroughly and press into the prepared pan.

*4* Bake in the preheated oven for 25 minutes. Let cool a little in the pan before turning out and slicing. Serve hot or cold with steamed green vegetables.

## variation

Add a colorful filling—fill the pan halfway with the nut mixture, then add a layer of chopped sun-dried tomatoes, chopped roasted red bell peppers, and chopped fresh herbs, then add the rest of the nut mixture and bake as in step 4.

# artichoke & tomato pie

## ingredients

### serves 6

1 tablespoon olive oil, plus extra
    for greasing
1 onion, sliced
2 garlic cloves, finely chopped
½ cup coarsely chopped
    sun-dried tomatoes in oil
8 artichoke hearts in oil,
    coarsely chopped
1 tablespoon chopped fresh
    tarragon
1 teaspoon tomato paste
¼ cup vegan dry white wine
1 package vegan ready-to-bake
    puff pastry
all-purpose flour, for dusting

## method

1 Preheat the oven to 400°F and lightly grease
   a baking sheet.

2 Heat the oil in a large skillet over medium heat. Sauté
   the onion for 5 minutes, or until softened. Stir in the
   garlic, sun-dried tomatoes, artichoke hearts, tarragon,
   tomato paste, and wine. Mix everything together well
   and cook for an additional 5 minutes. Remove from the
   heat and let cool for 5 minutes.

3 Place the puff pastry sheet on a floured surface. Using
   a sharp knife, cut two circles, one 9 inches in diameter
   and one 8 inches in diameter.

4 Place the smaller circle of pastry on the prepared
   baking sheet and top with the filling, leaving a 1-inch
   border around the edge. Put the larger circle of pastry
   on top, press the edges together firmly to seal, and
   then fold in the edge and crimp decoratively with your
   fingers or a fork. Using the tip of a sharp knife, make a
   little hole in the top of the pie to let steam escape.

5 Bake in the preheated oven for 20 minutes, or until
   golden. Serve immediately.

# hot tofu fajitas

## ingredients

*serves 4*

**fajita spice**
¼ teaspoon garlic powder
¼ teaspoon onion powder
¼ teaspoon cayenne pepper
¼ teaspoon dried oregano
¼ teaspoon ground allspice
1 tablespoon all-purpose flour

7 ounces firm tofu
3 tablespoons vegetable oil
1 onion, thickly sliced
1 red bell pepper, seeded
    and sliced
1 yellow bell pepper, seeded
    and sliced
4 soft vegan tortillas, warmed
salsa and lime wedges, to serve

## method

*1* Drain the tofu and press with paper towels to remove any excess water. Cut into slices about ½ inch thick.

*2* Combine the fajita spice ingredients in a small bowl and spread onto a large plate. Dip the tofu into the spices, coating both sides of each slice with the mixture.

*3* Heat 2 tablespoons of the vegetable oil in a large skillet over medium heat. Cook the tofu slices for 5 minutes, turning carefully once or twice, until browned and crisp.

*4* In a small bowl, toss the onion and bell peppers in the remaining vegetable oil. Sauté in a hot ridged grill pan for 6–8 minutes. Try not to move the vegetables too often, so that you get some distinctive stripes.

*5* Serve the warm tofu and the vegetables in bowls with the tortillas on separate plates, letting everybody assemble their own fajita. Serve with salsa and lime wedges, for squeezing over the fajitas.

# smoky mushroom burgers

## ingredients

### serves 6

1 (15-ounce) can red kidney
  beans, drained and rinsed
2 tablespoons sunflower oil or
  vegetable oil, plus extra for
  brushing
1 onion, finely chopped
2 cups finely chopped mushrooms
1 large carrot, shredded
2 teaspoons smoked paprika
¾ cup rolled oats
3 tablespoons dark soy sauce
2 tablespoons tomato paste
⅔ cup chopped fresh cilantro
  (including stems)
3 tablespoons all-purpose flour
salt and pepper, to taste

### to serve

vegan hamburger buns
lettuce
sliced avocado
tomato salsa or relish

## method

1 Place the beans in a large bowl and mash thoroughly with a potato masher. Heat the oil in a skillet, add the onion, and sauté for 2 minutes, until translucent. Add the mushrooms, carrot, and paprika and sauté for an additional 4 minutes, until the vegetables are soft.

2 Add the fried vegetables to the beans with the oats, soy sauce, tomato paste, and cilantro. Season with salt and pepper and mix well. Divide into six equal portions and shape into patties, then turn in the flour to coat lightly.

3 Preheat a ridged grill pan until smoking. Lightly brush the tops of the patties with oil, then place, oiled side down, on the pan. Cook over medium heat for 2–3 minutes, until lightly charred underneath. Lightly brush the tops with oil, turn, and cook for an additional 2–3 minutes on the other side. Serve hot in soft buns with lettuce, avocado slices, and salsa.

# desserts

# fruit salad with ice cream

## ingredients

*serves 4*

### ice cream

2 tablespoons arrowroot powder
1 cup soy milk
2 cups soy cream
¾ cup vegan granulated sugar
1 tablespoon vanilla extract

### fruit salad

2–3 cups mixed soft fruit
(strawberries, raspberries,
blueberries, peaches,
nectarines, kiwis)
fresh mint leaves, to garnish

## method

*1* In a small bowl, mix the arrowroot with enough soy milk to make a smooth, runny mixture and set aside.

*2* Put the remaining soy milk, soy cream, and sugar into a large saucepan and bring to a boil, stirring to be sure that the sugar is dissolved. Once boiling point is reached, take the pan off the heat and stir in the arrowroot mixture and the vanilla extract. Let cool.

*3* Transfer to an ice cream maker and churn, according to the manufacturer's directions. Alternatively, pour the cooled mixture into a shallow freezerproof container and place in the freezer. Let freeze until not quite set, then take out of the freezer, stir, and freeze again until firm.

*4* Rinse or peel the fruit and chop into bite-size pieces, if preferred. Serve with the ice cream, garnished with one or two fresh mint leaves.

# sparkling wine sorbet

## ingredients

*serves 4*

¾ cup vegan granulated sugar
⅔ cup water
thinly pared strip of lemon zest
juice of 1 lemon
1½ cups vegan sparkling wine
grapes and fresh mint sprigs,
    to decorate

## method

**1** Place the sugar and water in a saucepan with the lemon zest. Stir over low heat until the sugar dissolves, then boil for 2–3 minutes to reduce by half. Let cool and remove the lemon zest.

**2** Combine the syrup with the lemon juice and wine, then churn the mixture in an ice cream maker following the manufacturer's directions. Alternatively, pour the cooled mixture into a shallow freezerproof container and freeze, uncovered, whisking at hourly intervals until frozen.

**3** When ready to serve, let stand at room temperature to soften slightly, then scoop the sorbet into sundae glasses. Decorate with grapes and mint sprigs.

# raw chocolate ice cream

## ingredients

*serves 4*

3 bananas

3 tablespoons raw unsweetened cocoa powder

1 tablespoon agave nectar

## method

*1* Peel the bananas and cut them into ¾-inch pieces. Place in a freezer bag and freeze for 3 hours.

*2* Take the bananas from the freezer and place in a food processor or blender with the cocoa powder and agave nectar. Process until smooth. Serve immediately or refreeze for a firmer consistency.

# green tea & hazelnut ice cream

## ingredients

*serves 6*

1¾ cups canned coconut milk
2½ cups fresh finely grated
    coconut
1 cup vegan superfine or
    granulated sugar
1 tablespoon green tea powder
½ cup roasted hazelnuts, chopped

## method

**1** Place the coconut milk and grated coconut in a medium saucepan over medium heat and mix together.

**2** Whisk in the sugar and green tea powder and heat until the sugar has dissolved. Stir in the chopped hazelnuts and set aside to cool to room temperature.

**3** Transfer to an ice cream maker and churn according to the manufacturer's ditrections. Alternatively, pour the cooled mixture into a shallow freezerproof container and place in the freezer. Let freeze until not quite set, then remove from the freezer, stir, and freeze again until firm. Store in the freezer until required.

# baked plums with port

## ingredients

*serves 4*

8 large plums
1 cinnamon stick
2 strips pared orange rind
2 tablespoons packed vegan light
    brown sugar
2 tablespoons light agave nectar
1 cup vegan port

## method

1 Preheat the oven to 350°F. Halve and pit the plums.

2 Place the plum halves, cut side up, in a small baking dish with the cinnamon stick and orange rind. Sprinkle with the sugar. Mix together the agave and port and pour around the plums.

3 Bake in the preheated oven for 30–40 minutes, or until the plums are soft. Let cool for 5 minutes, then pour off the liquid into a small saucepan.

4 Bring the liquid to a boil, then simmer for 5–10 minutes, or until syrupy and reduced by about one third. Pour the syrup over the plums. Serve immediately.

# coconut rice pudding

## ingredients

*serves 4*

5 cardamom pods
½ cup short-grain rice
2½ cups soy milk
1¾ cups coconut milk
¼ cup vegan granulated sugar
pinch of saffron
2 tablespoons slivered almonds

## method

1 Crack open the cardamom pods and remove the seeds. Crush the seeds in a mortar and pestle or with a rolling pin. Place the rice, soy milk, coconut milk, sugar, crushed cardamom seeds, and saffron in a large saucepan over low heat. Simmer for 40 minutes, stirring frequently, until the mixture is thick and creamy.

2 Toast the slivered almonds in a dry skillet over high heat for 2–3 minutes, or until lightly golden.

3 Serve the rice pudding hot or cold, topped with the toasted almonds.

# blueberry strudel

## ingredients

*serves 4–6*

1½ cups blueberries
1 tablespoon cornstarch
½ cup vegan granulated sugar
all-purpose flour, for dusting
6 sheets vegan phyllo pastry
¼ cup vegan margarine, melted
    and cooled
vegan confectioners' sugar, to serve

## method

*1* Preheat the oven to 375°F. Line a baking sheet with parchment paper.

*2* In a medium bowl, mix together the blueberries, cornstarch, and sugar.

*3* Place two sheets of phyllo pastry on a floured board, overlapping them slightly. Brush them with melted margarine and cover with two more sheets. Brush these with margarine and top with an additional two sheets of pastry.

*4* Place the fruit mixture in a line close to one long edge of the pastry. Starting at that edge, carefully roll up the pastry, folding in the ends as you roll.

*5* Transfer the strudel to the prepared baking sheet, brush the surface with the remaining melted margarine, and bake in the preheated oven for 20 minutes, or until golden. Dust with confectioners' sugar before serving warm or cold.

# spiced squash tarts

## ingredients

*serves 4*

3 cups diced butternut squash
(½-inch pieces)
1½ teaspoons vegan margarine,
melted, plus extra for greasing
1 tablespoon maple syrup
1 piece preserved ginger in syrup,
finely chopped
¼ teaspoon cinnamon
¼ teaspoon allspice
8 sheets vegan phyllo pastry
2 tablespoons canola oil
vegan confectioners' sugar, to
serve

## method

*1* Preheat the oven to 375°F. Lightly grease four 4-inch tart pans.

*2* Place the squash on a baking sheet and dot with the margarine. Roast in the preheated oven for 5 minutes, then stir and return to the oven for an additional 20 minutes, or until the squash is beginning to brown. Stir in the maple syrup, chopped ginger, cinnamon, and allspice, and cook for an additional 5 minutes. Let cool.

*3* Cut the phyllo pastry into twelve 4-inch squares. Brush four with canola oil. Place a second sheet of pastry on top of each, at an angle to the first so that the points of the squares do not align—you are aiming to create a star shape. Brush with oil again and finish with the remaining pastry sheets to make four stacks, each with three layers. Transfer the pastry stacks into the prepared tart pans, press down gently, and bake for 8–10 minutes, or until crisp and golden.

*4* Fill the pastry shells with the squash mixture. Dust with confectioners' sugar and serve immediately.

# baked apples

## ingredients

*serves 4*

4 cooking apples, such as Pippin, Rome, or Jonagold
1 tablespoon lemon juice
⅓ cup blueberries
⅓ cup raisins
¼ cup mixed nuts, chopped and toasted
½ teaspoon ground cinnamon
2 tablespoons vegan brown sugar
1 cup vegan red wine
2 teaspoons cornstarch
4 teaspoons water

## method

1 Preheat the oven to 400°F. Using a sharp knife, score a line around the center of each apple. Core the apples, then brush the centers with the lemon juice to prevent discoloration. Transfer them to a small roasting pan.

2 Place the blueberries and raisins in a bowl, then add the nuts, cinnamon, and sugar. Mix together well. Pile the mixture into the centers of the apples, then pour the wine over them.

3 Transfer the stuffed apples to the preheated oven and bake for 40–45 minutes, or until tender. Remove from the oven, then lift the apples out of the roasting pan and keep them warm.

4 Blend the cornstarch with the water, then add the mixture to the cooking juices in the roasting pan. Transfer to the stove and cook over medium heat, stirring, until thickened. Remove from the heat and pour it over the apples. Serve immediately.

# raspberry chocolate cake

## ingredients

### serves 12

vegan margarine, for greasing
2⅓ cups all-purpose flour
½ cup unsweetened cocoa powder
1 teaspoon baking powder
1 teaspoon baking soda
½ teaspoon salt
1½ cups vegan granulated sugar
1½ cups soy milk
½ cup canola oil
½ cup raspberry jelly
    or raspberry preserves, warmed
    and strained
1 teaspoon vanilla extract

### frosting

3 tablespoons soy milk
3 ounces vegan semisweet
    chocolate, broken into
    small pieces
½ cup vegan confectioners' sugar
1 tablespoon maple syrup
fresh raspberries, to decorate

## method

*1* Preheat the oven to 350°F. Grease a 9-inch cake pan and line with parchment paper.

*2* Sift the flour, cocoa, baking powder, and baking soda into a large mixing bowl and stir in the salt and sugar. Pour the soy milk into a medium saucepan and add the oil, raspberry jelly, and vanilla extract. Place over medium heat and whisk to combine. Stir into the dry ingredients and mix thoroughly.

*3* Transfer to the prepared cake pan and bake in the preheated oven for 45 minutes, or until a toothpick inserted into the center comes out clean. Let cool completely on a wire rack before frosting.

*4* To make the frosting, heat the soy milk in a small saucepan over medium heat until it reaches boiling point, then add the chocolate to the pan and stir until completely melted. Remove from the heat and whisk in the confectioners' sugar and maple syrup. Set aside to cool before frosting the cake, using a spatula. Top with a few fresh raspberries before slicing and serving.

## variation

For a chocolate and orange cake, substitute orange marmalade for the raspberry jelly and decorate with segmented oranges dipped in melted vegan chocolate.

# mixed berry bundt cake

## ingredients

*serves 12*

2¾ cups all-purpose flour,
    plus extra for dusting
2 teaspoons baking powder
1 teaspoon baking soda
2 cups vegan granulated sugar
¾ cup dry unsweetened coconut
2 cups soy milk
⅔ cup canola oil,
    plus extra for greasing
2 teaspoons vanilla extract
1 teaspoon salt
2 cups mixed berries, such as
    raspberries, blueberries, and
    blackberries, plus extra to serve
vegan confectioners' sugar, to dust
vegan vanilla ice cream, to serve
    (optional)

## method

1 Preheat the oven to 350°F. Grease and flour a 9½-inch bundt pan.

2 Sift together the flour, baking powder, and baking soda into a large bowl and stir in the sugar and coconut. Add the soy milk, oil, and vanilla extract. Beat together until smooth—the mixture will look like a thick batter. Stir in the salt and berries.

3 Pour the batter into the bundt pan. Bake in the preheated oven for 1 hour, or until a toothpick inserted into the cake comes out clean. Let cool in the pan for 5 minutes before turning out onto a wire rack.

4 When the cake has cooled, dust it with confectioners' sugar and fill the center with more fresh berries. Slice and serve with a scoop of vegan vanilla ice cream, if desired.

# boozy berry pudding

## ingredients

*serves 6*

4 cups mixed blueberries, raspberries, and red or black currants, plus extra to decorate

3–4 tablespoons vegan granulated sugar

⅓ cup vegan port

1 pint strawberries, hulled and halved or quartered if large

6–7 slices vegan thick white bread, crusts removed

## method

*1* Place the mixed fruit, 2 tablespoons of the sugar, and half of the port in a saucepan over low heat. Simmer gently for 3–4 minutes, until the fruit starts to release its juices. Remove from the heat. Add the strawberries and stir in the remaining sugar to taste.

*2* Line a 1-quart deep, round bowl with plastic wrap, letting the ends overhang. Transfer the fruit into a strainer set over a separate bowl to catch the juices, then stir the remaining port into the juices. Cut a circle the same size as the bottom of the lined bowl out of one slice of bread. Dip in the juice mixture and place in the bottom of the lined bowl.

*3* Reserve one slice of bread. Cut the rest in half slightly on an angle. Dip the pieces one at a time in the juice mix and place around the sides of the lined bowl, pushing them together so there are no gaps and trimming the final piece to fit. Fill with the fruit, then cover with the reserved piece of bread, cut to fit the top. Put a small plate on top and weigh it down with a can of beans. Chill overnight. Refrigerate any remaining juice.

*4* Remove the weight and plate, then cover the dessert with a serving plate and flip over. Remove the bowl and plastic wrap and decorate with extra fruit. Serve with any remaining juice.

# tropical fruit skewers

## ingredients

*makes 8*

**rum sauce**
¼ cup orange juice
3 or 4 strips of orange zest
3 or 4 strips of lemon zest
½ cup vegan dark rum
2 tablespoons vegan dark
    brown sugar
3 cardamom pods, cracked open

selection of tropical fruit (melon,
    star fruit, orange, kiwi,
    pineapple, banana, mango)

## method

1 Put all of the ingredients for the rum sauce into a small saucepan. Place over low heat and simmer for 10–15 minutes, or until reduced by half. Use a slotted spoon to remove the zest and cardamom pods. Set aside to reheat when you are ready to serve the skewers.

2 Rinse or peel the fruit and cut into large pieces. If you are using wooden skewers, presoak them in water for 10 minutes before making up the skewers. Assemble eight skewers, allowing 8–10 pieces of fruit per skewer.

3 Preheat the broiler to high. Place the skewers under the preheated broiler or on a barbecue, turning frequently, until browning and heated through. Serve immediately with the rum sauce.

# peanut butter cups

## ingredients

*makes 30*

¼ cup creamy peanut butter
2 tablespoons vegan margarine
¼ cup vegan confectioners' sugar
12 ounces vegan semisweet
　　chocolate, broken into pieces

## method

1 Line a miniature muffin pan with 30 miniature paper liners.

2 Place the peanut butter and 1 tablespoon of the margarine in a small nonmetallic bowl. Microwave for 30 seconds to 1 minute, or until softened but not melted. Mix in the confectioners' sugar thoroughly.

3 Place the chocolate and the remaining margarine in a double boiler or a large heatproof bowl set over a saucepan of simmering water. Stir until completely melted.

4 Put a teaspoonful of melted chocolate into each paper liner, top with half a teaspoon of the peanut butter filling, and cover the filling with more melted chocolate. Be careful to avoid overfilling the paper liners. Chill in the refrigerator for 1 hour, or until firm.

# pecan & cranberry pie

## ingredients

*serves 6*

### dough

¼ cup packed vegan margarine

1¼ cups all-purpose flour, plus extra for dusting

2 tablespoons vegan confectioners' sugar

### filling

¼ cup dried cranberries

grated rind and juice of 1 orange

1 tablespoon vegan brandy (optional)

1 cup pecans

⅔ cup maple syrup

½ cup soy milk

3 tablespoons vanilla extract

1 teaspoon cinnamon

1 teaspoon ginger

1 teaspoon flaxseed meal (ground flaxseeds)

## method

1 Preheat the oven to 375°F.

2 Place the cranberries in a small bowl with the orange juice and brandy, if using. Set aside for at least an hour to plump up.

3 To make the dough, rub the margarine into the flour in a large mixing bowl, then stir in the confectioners' sugar. Gradually add enough cold water to make a soft dough. Roll the dough out on a floured board and use it to line an 8-inch tart pan. Put the pecans into the pastry shell and bake in the preheated oven for 15 minutes.

4 Put the maple syrup, soy milk, vanilla extract, cinnamon, ginger, and orange rind into a medium saucepan over low heat. Simmer gently for 5 minutes then remove from the heat.

5 Remove the pastry shell from the oven but keep the oven on. Use a slotted spoon to remove the cranberries from the soaking liquid and arrange them on top of the pecans. Stir the flaxseed meal into the remaining soaking liquid and then stir this into the maple mixture.

6 Carefully pour the mixture into the pastry shell. Return the pie to the oven for an additional 30 minutes. Let cool before slicing and serving.

# rhubarb & plum crisp

## ingredients

### serves 4

2½ cup chopped rhubarb
   (1-inch pieces)
½ cup vegan granulated sugar
7 ripe plums, halved and pitted
½ teaspoon cinnamon

### topping

½ cup chopped hazelnuts
⅓ cup packed vegan margarine
1¼ cup all-purpose flour
¼ cup vegan granulated sugar

## method

*1* Preheat the oven to 375°F.

*2* Place the rhubarb and ¼ cup of the granulated sugar in a large lidded saucepan. Place over low heat and cook, covered, for 5–8 minutes, or until tender.

*3* Transfer the rhubarb to an 8-inch square baking dish and spread the plums on top. Sift the remaining ¼ cup granulated sugar with the cinnamon and sprinkle over the fruit.

*4* To make the topping, toast the chopped hazelnuts in a dry skillet over high heat for 5 minutes, or until browned.

*5* In a large mixing bowl, rub the margarine into the flour to resemble large bread crumbs, then stir in the sugar and toasted nuts. Cover the fruit with the crumb topping and bake in the preheated oven for 25–30 minutes, or until browning and bubbling. Let cool for 5 minutes then serve immediately.